# Anxiety in Relationships

*How Anxiety Ruins Relationships and Why You NEED to Stop Feeling Insecure and Attached in Love. Learn to Identify Irrational Behaviors That Trigger Anxiety With Practical Strategies RIGHT NOW!*

# Table of Contents

# Introduction

Being in a relationship with someone when you have anxiety issues or an anxiety disorder can be in itself very depressing. Oftentimes, you may get the impression that anxiety is a third person in the relationship, an imaginary personality who comes in between you and your partner. This person is responsible for all the confusion and issues you experience in your relationship.

Anxiety can cause periods of panic, feelings of fear or a sense of being overwhelmed, uneasy, or tense. Anxiety can take over your thoughts and spread into many other areas of your life, thereby affecting your reasoning and productivity. It infuses a strain in relationships and puts them at great risk. When anxiety is thriving in a relationship, the trust and connection every relationship needs is broken. When anxiety sets in, it takes your mind off the most important aspects of your relationship, and you become less attuned to the needs and desires of your partner. Fear and worry become the order of the day.

You feel overwhelmed, worried about what is happening, but find it difficult to actually pay attention to what is happening. When this occurs, your partner may feel as though you are not present. When you are anxious in your relationship, you may find it difficult to express your true feelings. If you don't express what you truly feel or need, anxiety becomes more intense and your emotions may begin to run out of control if you keep bottling them in. This leads to you feeling overwhelmed and defensive.

Intimate relationships are able to reflect the best and worst of us all. They are mirrors that can fuel our struggles or calm them. Anxiety is a poison that can steal the joy and connection between two people who belong together. Perhaps you have been with your partner for a long period of time, yet you constantly wrestle with the notion that your partner doesn't live up to your expectations and will not be able to fill up that void in your heart.

Maybe you also suspect that you are a part of the problem. Perhaps you are insecure in love; you feel terribly lonely and desire a companion and lover to accompany you through the adventure and journey of life. You constantly wonder if anyone would be truly there for you if you let down your guard and are yourself. Would you be able to find comfort, reassurance, and support from them in your vulnerability? You ponder over these things at every opportunity.

The main goal of this book is to let you know that you can overcome whatever anxiety you have faced or are currently going through in your relationships. A lot of people like you have been able to face their fears, look it in the eye, and conquer every anxiety and limiting force blocking their joy. This book is not only for couples or romantic partners; it is also for singles that look forward to a wholesome and healthy relationship in the future.

This book is a guide with practical strategies and exercises you can relate to that will help you on your growth and healing journey.

When you consciously implement all that has been written in this book and take all the exercises to heart, you will have conquered a large part of the anxiety that has been ruining your relationships. You will begin to feel less insecure and attached in love. By reading this book, you will be able to identify irrational behaviors that trigger anxiety and take concrete and positive steps to eliminate those behaviors.

I want you to know that you can enjoy a healthy, wholesome, and valuable love life, a relationship in which you are not needy and don't feel insecure or attached. You can have a loving relationship in which you see yourself growing and adding positive value, with your partner doing the same.

You will understand your relationship struggles as you flip through the pages of this book, and this is also an opportunity for you to discover your potential. You are worthy of great love, valuable love, quality and unending love, a love so true and pure it will stand the test of time. You will be able to identify the obstacles to nurturing happy relationships and how to avoid these obstacles. Through self-awareness, you will be able to develop a more secure and intimate relationship with your partner and lover.

This book will also help you light up your love life and keep your heart and mind full of love, peace, security, and value. To make the most of this book, take your time to read it, make notes as you read each page, and treat it as a guide and commit all the exercises and strategies to heart. You will surely see positive changes in your relationships if you put your all into conquering anxiety. Keep a journal to document your thoughts as you read, and write down your next course of action pertaining to your relationships. Let's get started, and good luck on your journey to a better life!

# Chapter 1: Anxiety and Insecurity

# in Relationships

Anxiety is a real challenge as well as a mental health disorder, which can lead to a lot of other problems if not properly checked. However, everyone develops anxiety from time to time, and it only becomes an issue if it is severe.

Anxiety can impact your relationships negatively, especially if you spend a great deal of time worrying and thinking about everything that could go wrong or has already gone wrong with the relationship. Here are some questions that may run through your mind when you are too anxious in a relationship:

What if they don't love me as much as I love them?

What if they're lying to me?

What if they're cheating on me?

What if I'm not good enough in the future for them?

What if they find someone else more attractive?

What if their family doesn't love me?

What if they die?

What if my anxiety ruins our relationship? (Anxiety about anxiety)

What if we break up?

What if they bail out on me?

It is normal to have some of these thoughts, especially in a new relationship. However, when thoughts like these come to your mind frequently, it might be a sign of anxiety issues or an anxiety disorder. The intensity with which you constantly ruminate over the questions listed above and other questions that are similar determine how far gone you are into an anxiety problem. It will also determine how insecure you are in your relationship.

These anxious thoughts are manifested in diverse physical ways and present as symptoms such as shortness of breath, insomnia, and anxiety or panic attacks. You may discover that whenever you think this way, you trigger a panic attack in which your heart may begin to beat fast, a hard lump forms in your chest, and you begin to shake all over your body. These are the physiological signs that you are suffering from an anxiety disorder.

In some cases, these anxious thoughts encourage your partner to behave in ways that further stress you out and strain the relationship. This is because you are transparent enough to your partner that they can see you are very insecure. This gives them a manipulative edge over you, to twist and turn events in ways that normally should not mean a thing but will eventually hurt you and confirm one or two of the anxious beliefs you have.

For example, you are worried and anxious about being the first to initiate a conversation all the time. You become sick in your mind that your partner doesn't like you because they don't take the first step in communicating as often as you do. The anxiety builds up and gathers momentum, and you begin to believe they might never chat with you or call you up if you do not reach out first.

To address this anxiety, you decide it is a good idea to go mute on them for a while. This forces your partner to communicate with you, reaching out a few times until you feel reassured knowing they will make the effort. This evidence allows you to challenge your anxious, irrational belief that they will not reach out first. This, however, is not a healthy strategy. Dealing with the root cause of anxiety and regaining your confidence is the best way to overcome anxiety disorder and leave you with a free and joyful life.

Intimate relationships are emotionally intense. This is due to the closeness that you share with another person. Alas, that closeness makes you powerless at times and can lead to anxiety and insecurity. Anxiety is fear of the unknown, while insecurity is self-doubt and the absence of self-confidence. Most times, insecurity graduates into anxiety if not properly managed.

It is also important to note that when you worry constantly in your relationship, you develop low self-esteem and ultimately insecurity sets in. You begin to see your partner's intentions or actions in a negative light; you view your partner as intimidating or critical.

Some symptoms of intense anxiety disorder can include:

- A feeling of restlessness

- Tensed muscles

- Difficulty concentrating or remembering

- Procrastinating or having trouble making decisions

- Worry that leads to repeatedly asking for reassurance

- Inability to get enough sleep and rest

Inasmuch as relationships are very beautiful and pleasurable, they can also breed anxious thoughts and feelings. These thoughts can arise at any stage of the relationship. If you aren't in a relationship yet, the thought of meeting the right person and being in a relationship can already generate anxiety for you, which you must deal with.

Insecurity is an inner feeling of not being enough or feeling threatened in some way. We've all felt it at one time or the other. It's quite normal to have feelings of self-doubt once in a while, but chronic insecurity can ruin your success in life and destroy your romantic relationships.

Severe insecurity steals your peace and prevents you from being able to engage with your partner in a relaxed and authentic way. The resultant actions arising from insecurity may include jealousy, false accusations, snooping, lack of trust, and seeking reassurance and validation. These attributes are not conducive to a healthy relationship and can push your partner away.

Most people believe that insecurity stems from the

actions or inaction of their partners. The reality is that most insecurity comes from within you. You build insecurity when you negatively compare yourself to other people and judge yourself harshly with your inner critical voice. A lot of the insecurities in your relationship are based on irrational thoughts and fears that you are not good enough and that you are not capable of making someone else happy. But these aren't true!

When you start to notice that uneasy feeling of being insecure, one thing you can do is to begin taking stock of your value. Insecurity makes you focus on something you feel is lacking within you. In most balanced relationships, each partner brings different strengths and qualities that complement each other. In order to conquer your insecurity, take stock of the value you offer to your partner. Personality and a great character are important qualities to the overall health of a relationship.

Building your self-esteem is also crucial to surmounting any insecurity you face in your relationship. It is important that you feel good about who you are on the inside in order to not constantly seek validation from someone else. You are complete within yourself and you must let your independence and self-worth shine brightly through your deeds and actions. When your well-being depends on someone else, you give them the key to your joy and you empower them. This may be quite unhealthy for your partner to bear and certainly does not work well for a relationship. One way to build your self-confidence is to silence your inner critic and focus your mind and attention on positive qualities. Look in the mirror and speak positive affirmations to yourself - looking yourself in the eye when you do this makes a greater impact than simply telling yourself in your head that you're worthy of love.

You should also be able to maintain your sense of self-identity and be able to cater to your personal well-being. If before the relationship you were doing a great job of tending to your physical, mental, and emotional needs, this should not stop now just because you are in a relationship. You should maintain your independence and not allow yourself to turn into someone who is needy or attached. Being an independent person who has a life and identity outside of the relationship also makes you a more interesting and attractive partner. Your life must continue to move forward and make considerable progress when you are in a relationship. Being in a relationship is not the final phase of your life, and you should continue to be driven and achieve more goals, which can further endear you to your partner.

Some ways to maintain your independence include cultivating and nurturing great friendships, making time for your own friends, interests, and hobbies, maintaining financial independence, constantly improving yourself, and setting high standards for your dreams.

## Understanding Why You Feel Anxious, Insecure and Attached in Relationships

When you begin a relationship, the initial stage can get you worried and tensed up with different questions in your head, begging for answers. You begin to think: "Does he/she really like me?" "Will this work out?" "How serious will this get?"

It is sad to know that these worries do not diminish in the later stages of the relationship when you're plagued with anxiety. As a matter of fact, the closer and more intimate you get in a relationship, the higher the intensity of the anxiety displayed in such a relationship can be.

Worry, stress, and anxiety about your relationships can leave you feeling lonely and dejected. You may unknowingly create a distance between yourself and your loved one. Another grave consequence of anxiety is its ability to make us give up on love completely. That is rather devastating, because love is a very beautiful thing. It is important to really understand what makes you so anxious in a relationship and why you feel so insecure and attached. I will take you through some of the reasons in subsequent paragraphs.

Falling in love puts a demand on you in countless ways - more ways than you can imagine. The more you cherish a person, the more you stand to lose. How ironic is that? This intense feeling of love and the powerful emotions that come with it consciously and unconsciously create the fear of being hurt and the fear of the unknown in you.

Oddly enough, this fear comes as a result of being treated exactly how you want to be treated in your relationship. When you begin to experience love as it should be, or when you are treated in tender and caring way which is unfamiliar to you, anxiety might sets in.

More often than not, it is not only the events that occur between you and your partner that lead to anxiety. It is the things you tell yourself and feed your mind with regarding those events that ultimately lead to anxiety. Your biggest critic, which is also the "mean coach" you have in your head, can criticize you and feed you with bad advice which will ultimately fuel your fear of intimacy. It is this mean critic that suggests to you that:

"You are not smart, he/she would soon get bored of you."

"You will never meet anyone who will love you, so why try?"

"Don't trust him, he's probably searching for a better person."

"She doesn't really love you. Get out before you get hurt."

This mean coach in your head manipulates you and turns you against yourself and the people you love. It encourages hostility, and you soon discover that you are paranoid. You begin to suspect every move your partner makes, and this reduces your self-esteem and drives unhealthy levels of distrust, defensiveness, jealousy, anxiety, and stress.

What this mean coach in your head does is constantly feed you with thoughts that jeopardize your happiness and make you worry about your relationship rather than allowing you to just enjoy it. When you begin to focus so much on these unhealthy thoughts, you become terribly distracted from the real relationship, which involves healthy communication and love with your partner.

You soon discover that you are reacting to unnecessary issues and uttering nasty and destructive remarks. You may also become childish or parental towards your partner.

For example, your partner comes home from work and does not have a good appetite, so they politely turn down dinner. Sitting alone after some time, your inner critic goes on a rampage and asks, "How can he refuse my food? What has he eaten all day? Who has been bringing food to him at work? Can I really believe him?" These thoughts can continually grow in your mind, until by the next morning you are insecure, furious, and temperamental. You may begin to act cold or angry, and this can put your partner off, making them frustrated and defensive. They won't know what's been going on in your head, so your behavior will seem like it comes out of nowhere.

In just a few hours, you have successfully shifted the dynamics of your relationship. Instead of savoring the time you are spending together, you may waste an entire day feeling troubled and drawn apart from each other. What you have just done is initiate and enthrone the distance you feared so much. The responsible factor for this turn of events is not the situation itself - it is that critical inner voice that clouded your thoughts, distorted your perceptions, suggested bad opinions to you and, as a result, led you to a disastrous path.

When it comes to the issues you worry about so much in your relationship, what you don't know - and what your inner critic doesn't tell you - is that you are stronger and more resilient than you think. The reality is that you can handle the hurts, rejections, and disappointments that you are so afraid of. We are made in such a way that it is possible to absorb negative situations, heal from them, and deal with them. You are capable of experiencing pain and ultimately healing and coming out stronger. However, the mean coach in your head, that inner critical voice, more often than not puts you under pressure and makes reality look like a tragedy. It creates scenarios in your head that are non-existent and brings out threats that are not tangible. Even when, in reality, there are real issues and unhealthy situations, that inner voice in your head will magnify such situations and tear you apart in ways you do not deserve. It will completely misrepresent the reality of the situation and dampen your own resilience and determination. It will always give you unpleasant opinions and advice.

These critical voices you hear in your head are, however, formed as a result of your own unique experiences and what you've adapted to over time. When you feel anxious or insecure, there is a tendency to become overly attached and desperate in our actions. Possessiveness and control towards your partner set in. On the other hand, you may feel an intrusion in your relationship. You may begin to retreat from your partner and detach from your emotional desires. You may begin to act unforthcoming or withdrawn.

These patterns of responding to issues may stem out of your early attachment styles. These style patterns influence how you react to your needs and how you go about getting them met.

There are some critical inner voices that talk about you, your partner, and your relationships. These inner voices are formed out of early attitudes you were exposed to in your family, amongst your friends, or in society at large. Everyone's inner critic is different; however, there are some common critical inner voices.

### Inner Voices that are Critical about the Relationship

- Most people end up getting hurt.

- Relationships never work out.

### Inner Voices that are Critical about Your Partner

- He's probably cheating on you.

- You can't trust her.

- Men are so insensitive, unreliable, and selfish.

### Inner Voices about Yourself

- You're better off on your own.

- It's your fault if he gets upset.

- You always screw things up.

- You have to keep him interested.

- He doesn't really care about you.

When you listen to your inner voice, the resultant effect is an anxiety filled relationship, which can mar your love life in many ways. When you give in to this anxiety, you may stop feeling like the strong and independent person you were when you first started the relationship. This can make you thin out and fall apart, which further induces jealousy and insecurity. Attachment and neediness set in, and these puts a strain on the relationship.

This anxiety disorder may begin to leave you feeling threatened in your relationship and you thus begin to dominate or control your partner. You find yourself setting rules for what they can or cannot do just to reduce your own insecurities. This may lead to a feeling of withdrawal and resentment from your partner.

When you allow yourself to be anxious in a relationship, you may begin to defend yourself by becoming cold and distant to protect yourself, and this can be traumatic for your partner. This distance can also stir up insecurity in your partner.

Sometimes, your response to anxiety is more akin to aggression. You may yell and scream at your partner without even realizing it. You have to consciously pay attention to how many of your actions are a direct response to your partner, and how often are they a response to your inner critical voice.

## Signs of Insecure Attachment

There are a few practices that are brought about by attachments as a result of insecurity. An assortment of undesirable practices can show in early adolescence as a result of unreliable connections.

### 1. Too Demanding

For instance, you don't want your partner to get things done without you. Your longing is to burn through the majority of your and their extra time together. You request their time and consideration, to the detriment of other friendships and relationships.

### 2. Doubt or Jealousy

For instance, you are suspicious of your partner or companion's conduct and the general population they work with. You question their work connections and who they communicate with in the work environment.

You are suspicious of anybody that you feel they are getting too close to, as you dread that they may leave you for another person.

### 3. Absence of Emotional Intimacy

For instance, your companion or partner feels that they sincerely can't draw near to you. They portray you as somebody who "sets up dividers" or say that you are commonly difficult to draw near to inwardly.

### 4. Enthusiastic Dependency

You rely upon your companion or partner for your enthusiastic prosperity. Your desire is that your joy originates from your relationship.

In the event that you are upset, this is on the grounds that you believe you aren't being satisfied by your partner or companion.

### 5. Frightful

You desire closeness in your personal connections. However, your experience has been that, in the event that you get excessively near your loved one, they will hurt you. This makes you have a blend of feelings.

You draw your partner close and subsequently push them away when it becomes "too much." Your dread of getting excessively close, since you would prefer not to be hurt, causes your relationship to suffer.

## 6. Absence of Trust

You don't confide in your companion out of fear that they may undermine you or leave you. You're afraid that you may tell them something or reveal a part of yourself that they won't like and will prompt them to end the relationship.

## 7. Anger Issues

Getting angry unnecessarily is also a sign of insecure attachment in a relationship. When you pick a fight over an issue that could be solved amicably, it shows that you are not ready to tolerate your partner or you are fed up of their excesses. This behavior, if not addressed, can affect the relationship adversely

Let me conclude by saying that when you act out your insecurities, you begin to push your partner away from you, thus creating a self-fulfilling prophecy. By self-fulfilling prophecy, I mean validating and giving life to those negative thoughts which come to your mind, also known as your inner voice. It begins to look like that voice was right after all. But no, it wasn't right. The struggle is internal and goes on regardless of the circumstances. When you live with anxiety, your life could in reality be like a fairy tale, but that inner voice will still have something negative to point out. It is important to deal with your insecurities without dragging your partner into them. You can do this by taking two steps:

1. Uncover the roots of your insecurities and find out what actually led to them.

2. Challenge the inner critical voice and mean coach that obstruct the free flow of love in your relationship.

# Chapter 2: Why You Act

# Irrationally

Love is just a big sprinkling of hormones in the brain which interrupt our normal way of behaving. It can feel crazy, distract us, and drive us wild. Love can be extremely tiring and awesomely beautiful all at the same time. When you are irrational, you are not able to listen to reason, logic, or apply common sense. You just want a particular need to be met, any way it can be.

Until that need is met, you act in terrific and unpredictable ways. What you must remember is that emotions form an important aspect of our lives, not only in influencing our wellness, but also in determining our relationships with people. There are times when negative emotions overwhelm you, despite how much you try to keep them in check. Emotions involve complex states of mind that affect the body as well as your external environment.

Your emotions are a perception of the events going on in and around you. These emotions cause you to portray one or more patterns of behavior. When you are upset by something or someone, you get angry and may lash out, and when something makes you overwhelmed and unhappy, you cry. In the same way, when you are experiencing the positive emotions of love, you may show affection and when something is funny, you express yourself by laughing.

The ability to both understand and control your emotional responses is an important skill that affects your relationship with others. If all you do is constantly express negative emotions, also known as negative energy, your relationships and even your health can be at great risk. Irrational behavior is a demonstration of intense emotion in a situation in which your partner does not understand why such strong emotion is necessitated.

Romantic relationships are an arena where emotions run wild, as do misunderstandings which are often caused by these emotions and their effects that lead to irrationality. The reason for this is because they are engaged in an attachment relationships.

Attached relationship, if approached in the right way, can foster love, security and comfort. However, if the partners are not alive and responsive to each other's need, this kind of relationship can be a turbulent one.

When you feel that the security of your relationship is threatened, you may respond with strong emotions such as grief, loneliness, anger, and disappointment. These responses, if intensely expressed, can seem irrational.

Science might not be able to tell you exactly what love is, however it will tell you what love will do. When in love, the sensory, molecular, and organic chemistry processes concerned as well as sexual union have the tendency to make people do foolish things.

Attraction, romantic feelings, and aroused love that sometimes happens within the first stages of a relationship are characterized by obsessive behavior, targeted attention, and intense desire. This is due to the fact that you are in high spirits when the relationship is going well - however, terrible mood swings follow when it is not.

This is the stage of affection when we see folks act the most irrational, impulsive, and emotional, showing direct similarities to the emotional mind frame of addiction.

The feeling of a real bond with somebody, or rather the sense of calm, peace, and stability that this bond causes, is attributed to the hormones that are discharged through childbirth, milk production, and orgasms.

So however sensible a couple's "chemistry" is, it will still have some rather dangerous behavioral and emotional results. Love is as natural to human life as breathing. Attempting to prevent it out of fear or discomfort is suffocating.

## Irrational Behaviors that are caused by Anxiety

Anxiety alters your brain chemistry and thus triggers behaviors and emotions that under normal circumstances would never even occur to you. However, when anxiety takes over, all bets are off. Here are some of the behaviors that can occur when an uncomfortable situation or stressful trigger crops up in your relationship:

### *Excessive, Obsessive Worrying*

We all worry - it's natural. Life is unpredictable, which is one of the reasons anxiety is so prevalent. However, when that worry begins to overtake your mind to the extent that you can't think about anything else, there's a problem.

You might, after seeing a suspicious text, feel a twinge of worry before thinking about the situation rationally. My partner loves me, I have complete trust in them, and I know that they will not hurt me. There's no reason to jump to conclusions.

Of course, if you're dealing with anxiety, this situation triggers more than a moment of worry. Your mind will suddenly be filled with bits and pieces of messages you've seen in the past, whether innocent or not, and you'll go over all of your partner's actions in your mind to try to identify and moments where you felt suspicious. Worry turns into panic, which leads you into the territory of the irrational. If you've seen many signs of cheating, it isn't irrational to worry. However, if this is the first and there has never been a spark of an indication in the past, that's when the behavior begins to look irrational. No matter the outcome, worrying to the point of panic will not give you the answers you seek. To stop worrying, you need to let go of the things you can't control.

### Unwarranted Irritability

We get irritated as humans. That's okay! You might have had a bad day, or you're hungry, or any of a dozen other reasons. Irritability isn't irrational until it's born from anxiety. The fight or flight response that kicks up all kinds of hormones can put us on edge, leading to excessive irritation from no cause other than anxiety. The unfortunate thing about irritability is that it's so easy to direct at loved ones. When irrational irritability springs up and causes you to lash out at your partner, it can be difficult to explain why you did so. You may not even know yourself where the mood is coming from, which can lead you to conclude that you're just mad at your partner for some reason and now seemed like a good time to express that anger. Your partner won't know what they did, and before you know it a rift has formed in your relationship. The cause of the initial anxiety is no longer of any concern, because the resulting irritation is what did all the damage.

### Physical Aggression

Again, the fight or flight response kicks into gear and triggers nearly automatic reactions, some of which are violent. When you feel threatened or in danger, your body takes over to protect you. When you're in a situation that makes you anxious, if the severity is high then you are more likely to express that anxiety in a physical way. To protect yourself emotionally, you arm yourself physically. It may not make perfect sense to you even though you're the one displaying the behavior - that's what makes it irrational.

## *Moping*

This might seem like a less drastic behavior than irritability or aggression, but it can be detrimental nonetheless. Moping is characterized by sadness, depression, and a lack of energy. This comes as a result of anxiety causing a shut down in your mind and body. Your limbs become lethargic, as does your mind, and this depression of the internal function causes sadness to emerge from seemingly nowhere. The only thought you may have is "I don't feel like it," no matter what "it" is. This depressive mood can strain a relationship, especially if your partner doesn't know if they did something wrong or why you're feeling the way you are. You may not even know.

### Compulsive Behavior

Anxiety is often at the root of obsessive compulsive disorder. You desire to be able to control some aspect of the world, so you develop routines and habits that offer you some semblance of order. The uncertainty found in relationships can lead to anxious thoughts about the future, so you engage in compulsive behaviors that give you a way to control a small part of your life and future. These behaviors can be almost anything, but some of the more common ones include checking the locks several times, ensuring the burner is off multiple times before leaving the house (even if the stove wasn't used), needing to keep everything straightened or in a specific order, and more.

### Agoraphobia

If you never leave the house, there are fewer things that will trigger your anxiety, right? Severe anxiety can lead to agoraphobia, or the fear of going somewhere that may lead to embarrassment or cause panic. Crowded places are particularly troublesome

36

to those afflicted. While it's irrational to always expect the worse, it's absolutely understandable. It's hard to put yourself out there, and this fear of the unknown can make you never want to leave the relative safety of home. Whether you have already met someone or would like to, it can be difficult to start or maintain a relationship when you never want to leave the house.

## Understanding Your Partner

The ability to understand your partner's emotional well-being is important to cultivating a healthy relationship. Once you are able to precisely identify an emotion your partner is expressing or the reason why your partner is behaving in a certain way, you can respond to their needs more effectively. This enables you to offer the appropriate kind of support and know the right things to say in the right situations.

The importance of understanding your partner's views, opinions, and perspective, especially during heated disagreements, cannot be overemphasized. You can develop a good understanding of your partner's emotions by regularly asking them how they are feeling, why they feel that way, and what that feeling can be compared with. This will go a long way in assisting you in times when you are not very certain of the emotions your partner is feeling or why they are expressing those particular emotions.

You should also be able to understand your feelings and get to a level of emotional stability in order for you to do a good job at understanding your partner's feelings. When you improve your emotional self-awareness, your partner will also be moved to do the same.

When it comes to emotions, you should recognize that it may not be very easy for your partner to express their emotions fully to you. The level of trust and confidence your partner has in you will inform how much of their feelings they will be able to share with you. A general sense of trust must be established in a relationship.

Effective communication is very important in understanding your partner. Be sure to communicate your feelings and thoughts as appropriately as possible. This will enhance greater trust and confidence in the relationship. Understanding is really one of the top qualities of a great partner in any romantic relationship, and everyone wants someone who tries to understand them.

You should also be careful about imposing your ideals and beliefs on your partner. It does not matter how much you think you are better than your partner in terms of experience, maturity, or even in intellect - you must never force you own view of the world on your partner. You should be able to respect their own point of view, ideas, and perspectives on life and situations in general.

One sure way to understand your partner and get the best out of the relationship is to understand and acknowledge that your relationship is not the center of the universe. This also applies to your partner. You must maintain and improve upon the life you were living before you started. You should not force your partner to prioritize your relationship and you should also give them freedom to live, have fun, and be happy, even if you are not around.

Let your partner have outings with their friends, allow them socialize, let them travel solo and live their own lives to the fullest, even in your absence. Encourage them to pursue self-development and their personal goals. Constantly push your partner to be more and to achieve greater heights. This will help your partner appreciate you more, feel more confident about the relationship, and ultimately increase the affection they have for you.

In order to effectively understand your partner, you should learn how to compromise. You must be willing to find common ground, which is also a part of making sacrifices. You do not always have to point out that you are right. Remember that both of you are in the same boat, running towards a common goal and to this end, you are not enemies but partners in progress.

Another beautiful way to get to understand your partner is by giving them the opportunity to explain themselves and their situations before reacting. You must be able to guard your heart and emotions diligently. When you think that your partner wronged you or made you upset, you should give them a chance to explain. Listen to their side of the story and don't be the one to always judge your partner. Talking calmly to your partner should always take the priority over anger and damaging emotional outbursts.

I know it can be quite challenging when you are trying to understand your partner, especially when you feel that they did something wrong. It hurts the most if you feel betrayed and let down. Regardless, you have to find the strength and love to listen, with full sincerity. You also need to trust your partner enough to let them take you through their intentions and motivations for their acts.

Relationship thrives when partners understand and tolerate each other. Rather than getting upset on some issues, you can choose to exhibit maturity. If your partner offends you, instead of picking up a fight, try and call him/her and explain how they have wronged you. Let them realize that you have forgiven them but just want them to know. Annoyance will only worsen the situation. So, let peace rain in your relationship by avoiding anger at all cost. Couples that have stayed together for many years have one thing in common, and what is it? – they have learnt to control their anger. Another secret of a long lasting relation I will like to share with you is that once you discover your partner is angry, never do anything that will provoke them further. Also, never respond to anger with anger. Do you get that?

Another point that I will like to stress hear is understanding. Yes, it matters a lot. Lack of understanding has been the major reason why most relationship fail. At the start of a relationship, whether you are newly married or dating, the first duty of each of you is study each other's behavior. Ask questions if you are in doubt, your partner will always be willing to open up to you. When you are aware of the likes and dislikes of your partner, it will be difficult to step on their toes. And, always learn from your mistake. If your partner offends you, never keep grudges, no matter the gravity of the offence. Your ability to forgive and settle things amicably each time you partner offends is one of the pillars of every relationship

Along this process, you should also encourage your partner to open up to you more, no matter the situation. Sometimes, people find it difficult to communicate their ideas and feelings into words. This can pose a challenge, especially in romantic relationships. In this kind of situation, you may have to exercise a lot of patience. It is helpful to encourage your partner to be open to discussing issues that concern your relationship. When you do this, you show them that you're willing to listen and see their side of things, which will help your relationship flourish.

Understanding people's emotions and feelings is not always simple, especially in relationships. Active communication is very important in a relationship. You have to make an effort to constantly be in tune with their emotions and state of mind. Sometimes, you may discover that your partner is upset for reasons even they may not understand, and they still expect you to understand them. Of course, you are not a mind reader; the way to go about this is to be calm and patient with them. Try to share a productive conversation with the goal being to understand one another instead of getting defensive or angry.

One sure way to douse all manner of tension is to not unleash all your worries at once to your partner. This can be very overwhelming and thus counterproductive. You should also know and remember that emotional connection is a two way street. You must put in considerable effort trying to understand your partner emotionally in order for the effort to be reciprocated by them.

If you both raise your voice, it will be tough to be relaxed and properly understand each other. You have to pay attention to the volume and tone of your voice. The moment your voice increases in pitch, it will be difficult to understand or listen to your partner. You should also take heed and pay attention to your body language and mannerisms. Your body language can affect the way your partner responds to you, and this can make it hard for them to understand what you really need. If you stand with your arms crossed, for example, you'll appear defensive and as if you're shutting them out. Your body should reflect your willingness to communicate.

Furthermore, you can also cultivate the habit of communicating daily about how you feel about any situation and the relationship in general. You do not have to wait until there is an issue before you try to communicate your feelings. Create an environment where it is okay to talk about your feelings. One great way to do this is to ask open ended questions. You could ask questions like "What was the best part of your day and why?" as opposed to "How was your day?" This way, your partner will be persuaded to share more, and this enables the both of you have more meaningful conversations.

By all means possible, you must not give in to the pressure of forcing your partner to change. No criticisms, no requests for change. You should instead let it be about how you feel. When you speak about your feelings, it is essential to focus on using them as a way of sharing your own experience and making it clear that you just want to be listened to and understood. Don't mount pressure, and don't apportion blame. You should also let them know that they do not need to "fix" anything. When your partner attempts to fix the situation, it can put a lot of pressure on them. Let them know you just want them to understand how you are feeling.

When it comes to communicating your emotions, you also need to be able to choose your time very wisely. You should consider your partner's mood and state of mind before initiating emotional conversations. It certainly is not a great time for a discussion when your partner is sleepy, has deadlines to meet at work, or is with friends. You should also keep in mind that we all don't communicate the same way. Figure out how your partner communicates and help them understand how you communicate, as well. You should also learn to connect with your partner only when you're stable and not overly emotional yourself. The best way to make your partner relate with you emotionally is to reduce how emotional you feel at that particular moment.

After all is said and done, it is also important for you to know that you can choose to write a note/letter to your partner about the way you are feeling if you can't quite put it into words. Doing this can give you time to really think about what you want to say and also give your partner the time to read and plan their response in a level-headed manner. You should also keep in mind that people have diverse emotional experience, and not every situation resonates with everyone. You just need to keep taking baby steps, and the both of you will be able to meet halfway. Keep communicating, no matter what. That is the key to better understanding each other and expressing emotions in a very clear and healthy way.

Practical Ways to get to know your Partner Better

### Go on a vacation together

If you would like to understand your partner's true inner workings, then go on a vacation together, even if it's only for the weekend. You might think you know them well, but you do not fully know someone until you've seen them in all their intricacies. For example, how they react to a seven-hour flight delay and major fatigue will tell you a lot.

Experiencing new things together can reveal interests you did not even recognize your partner had. Either in a positive or negative way, you will have gotten to know your partner better by the time you head home.

### Hang out with his or her oldest friends

Hanging out together with your partner's current and

old friends is one way to understand your partner. There is nothing quite like meeting friends from their past. Old friends who have been with us through pivotal parts of our lives bring out the best in us. You may see a different side of your partner when they're interacting with friends. It is a cute way to get a glimpse at their younger self and the person they are with those they're closest to.

### Take a trip to their hometown

If you did not grow up in the same city or close to one another, take a visit to each other's hometown. Strolling around your partner's home can help you see what formed them into the person they are today. People come alive in places that are dear and familiar to them. As with old friends, you'll see a side of your partner that may not have come out before.

### Be a better listener

Along with all of the above suggestions, check that you actually hear your partner. Many times, our partner offers up information that we have a tendency to fail to grasp in casual spoken communication. Practice the art of true active listening to catch it all.

### Try out each other's hobbies

Sure, you recognize your partner goes to a book club on weekday evenings. However, do you know what they are reading, or why they like the group so much? Accompany them and see what it's all about. Friendship depends on commonalities, and it's vital to have an interest, or at the very least knowledge of, your partner's passions.

### Create shared hobbies

Try to create a hobby for the both of you to enjoy together. This can be something involving other couples or groups, like intramural sports teams, a book club, or a cooking class, or something involving just the two of you, like amateur photography or furniture refinishing. Working on something together is a great way to promote closeness and intimacy.

### Check up on them -not in a suspicious way

Make it a habit to talk with one another every single day about life in general. Whether you talk about how your day went or what's happening in your future, consistent communication provides you with a tremendously valuable chance to be closer to them. Be willing to know how they feel concerning any issue, when you team up with your partner to tackle a problem, you get the issue solved faster. So what I am trying to pass across is that when you do things in common, you get to know your partner better.

### Spend a lot of quality time together

Getting enough couple time builds intimacy, opens communication, and strengthens your bond, which successively strengthens your relationship. Stay in, hang out, and visit one another. This uninterrupted alone time can permit you to find out more about them.

### Build a couple's trivia game

How's this for a cute idea? A couple's trivia game

involves index cards and a question/answer session. Each of you creates twenty five questions about yourselves. Topics may include favorite song, least favorite relative, biggest complaint, best activities, blood type, etc. Then get to talking and see what you discover about each other!

### *Be honest with one another*

You can't expect to understand your partner if they are not honest with you and vice versa. Work toward the kind of relationship where honesty is a way of life. Share your personal issues with your partner whether it concerns them or not.

Getting to know someone is one of the most exciting aspects of any relationship. Discovering both similarities and differences brings you both closer together and allows you to embrace new ways of thinking.

# Chapter 3: Self-Evaluation of Anxiety in a Relationship

How do you know you are anxious in a relationship? What are the signs that show that you are having a negative emotion concerning your relationship? What are the effects of anxiety on your relationship? All of these questions will be answered when you carry out what is called a self-evaluation of relationship anxiety. This chapter focuses on the self-evaluation of tension in a relationship. The essence of this is to evaluate the issue to put an end to it.

Anxiety can spring out at any time in a relationship. The fact is that everyone is vulnerable to this problem; the tendency to become anxious in a relationship increases as the bond becomes stronger. So, there is a need for everyone to carry out a self-evaluation.

Do you spend most of your time worrying about things that could go wrong in your relationship? Do you doubt if your partner really loves you? A sure sign of relationship anxiety is when you become worried all the time as a result of those question running through your mind.

For proper self-evaluation of this problem, you need to know the signs that show that you are already becoming anxious. Also, you need to weigh the causes and effect of this problem on your relationship. As I have said earlier, the purpose of evaluating is to address the problem before it develops. This chapter is structured to give you maximum benefit, and I will try to be as explicit as possible.

## How to Know if You Are Getting Anxious in a Relationship

You might be neck deep in relationship anxiety without really knowing, so this section will point out the symptoms of this problem to you. If you notice any the signs that will be mentioned below, you will benefit greatly from the self-evaluation process.

## 1. When you feel jealous of your partner

Take a cursory look at your behavior. Do you feel like breaking somebody's head when your partner is close to the opposite sex? Are you threatened by any friends of theirs who you fear may "steal" your partner away from you? This is jealousy, and it is one of the signs that you are feeling anxious in your relationship. Sometimes, you might even have the urge to test your spouse's commitment and love; this is an indication of anxiety triggered by jealousy.

## 2. When your self-esteem is low

When you are always cautious of how you behave because you don't know what your partner's reaction will be, or you can't express yourself freely in front of your partner due to fear of rejection, this is an indication of low self-esteem - a sign that you are anxious in your relationship.

## 3. Lack of trust

Your partner is one of the people you should trust the

most. If you always have to confirm whatever your wife, husband, boyfriend, or girlfriend says before you believe them, it shows that there's a lack of trust in the relationship. Many times, the lack of trust is caused by past betrayal. However, you should not allow past betrayals to impact negatively on your relationship, provided they were one time occurrences. Realize that your partner is not perfect, and once they have assured you that such incidences will never happen again, believe them.

## 4. Emotional imbalance

Today you are frustrated, tomorrow you are angry, the next day you are happy – this is emotional instability. You might not be aware of this, but constant mood swings are also a sign of emotional imbalance, and they do not help the matter. They only worsen it. Whatever problems or issues you are facing, discuss them with your partner. When the two of you deliberate on a problem, you will get it solved quickly. When you discover that your mood is not stable, it is a symptom of anxiety in a relationship.

## 5. Lack of sleep and reduced sex drive

The aftermath of constant worry is insomnia, which is the inability to sleep, and when you are unable to sleep, your body is stressed, leading to decreased libido.

If you are experiencing one or more of these symptoms, what you need to do is to figure out the possible causes and deal with it. I am going to give you examples of likely causes of these problems.

## Possible Causes of a Relationship Anxiety

Most times, relationship anxiety could be a manifestation of a deep-rooted problem. Here are the common causes of relationship anxiety:

## 1. Complicated Relationship

When you are uncertain about your relationship, or it is not clearly defined, it can be classified as complicated. This applies to those that are dating. For instance, a woman may not know the intentions of the man - whether he wants to marry her or is just in it for fun. Also, a long distance relationship could result in anxiety. In such cases, partners must learn to trust each other.

## 2. Comparison

Comparing your current relationship with past ones should be avoided as much possible. You might begin to entertain feelings of regret if you discover that your previous relationship was better in the areas of finance, communication, sex, and other aspects. To avoid this feeling, you should never compare your marriage or relationship to that of others or the ones you have had in the past.

## 3. Constant fighting

When you are always quarreling with your partner, you might never stop worrying because you don't know when the next altercation will crop up. This is one of the causes of severe anxiety in a relationship, because your bid to avoid quarreling will not allow you to have a pleasant time with your partner.

## 4. Lack of understanding

Partners that do not take the time to understand each other will always face difficulties. As mentioned earlier, the constant quarreling will result in an anxious relationship. Are you noticing the symptoms of anxiety coupled with miscommunications? Lack of understanding might be the reason for your relationship anxiety. Get to know your partner better, and encourage them to know you.

## 5. Other issues

Difficult experiences in past unhealthy relationships might result in many other issues. Not only that, neglect during childhood, abuse in the past, and lack of affection are some of the reason why someone can feel anxious in a relationship.

Once you have identified the root cause of your relationship issue, getting rid of it will be the next step. Do not forget, the primary reason for the self-evaluation of any problem is to get rid of it. In the next section, we are going to examine the effect of anxiety on a relationship with logical steps towards putting an end to it.

## Effects of Anxiety on Relationships and How to stop it

This is a relevant section that you need to read carefully, as it opens your eyes to how anxiety manifests in a relationship and the effective ways to stop it no matter the way it appears.

### 1. Anxiety makes you continuously worry about your relationship

Persistent worry is one of the manifestations of relationship anxiety. If you are continually having thoughts such as, "Is my partner mad at me, or are they pretending to happy with me? Will this relationship last?" These kinds of views indicate one thing – WORRY. If you discover that you regularly entertain these kinds of thought, do the following:

- Clear your mind and live in the moment

- If negatives thoughts are continually running

through your mind, then stop, clear your mind, and think about the beautiful moments you have shared with your partner. Think about the promises your partner has made, and reassure yourself that your relationship is going to stand the test of time.

- Do not react impulsively - think before you take any step. Share your feelings with your partner rather than withdrawing from them - make an effort to connect.

## 2. Anxiety breeds mistrust

Anxiety makes you think negatively about your partner. You will find it difficult to believe anything they say. In some cases, you may suspect that your partner is going out with another person. These kinds of feelings inevitably come between you and your partner. It makes it hard for you to relate to them well. To put an end to this, follow these practical steps:

- Ask yourself, "Do I have any proof of my suspicion?"

- Go to your partner and talk things over with them

- Start again if you notice that your relationship is suffering from a lack of trust

- Reestablish the trust, date each other as if it is your first time, and gradually build the trust

- Do the things you did when you first met each other

### 3. Anxiety leads to self-centeredness

What anxiety does is take all your attention, making you focus solely on the problem while every other thing suffers. You don't have time for your partner; you are withdrawn to yourself. You focus mainly on yourself and neglect the physical and emotional needs of your partner. Here are the things to do to get rid of this attitude:

- Rather than magnifying and focusing on your fear, pay attention to your needs

- You can seek the support of your partner when you discover that you cannot handle the fear alone

## 4. Anxiety inhibits expression with your partner

Anything that stops you from expressing your sincere feeling to your partner is an enemy of your relationship. Anxiety is the culprit here; it hinders you from opening your mind to your partner. You think that they might rebuff you, or that telling them how you feel may cause an adverse reaction from them. This makes you keep procrastinating, instead of discussing the critical issues right away with them. How do you overcome the fear of rejection? Consider the following quick steps:

- Focus on the love your partner has for you

- Voice out what you feel to get rid of anxiety

- Approach your partner cheerfully

- Discuss heartily with them

## 5. Anxiety makes you sad

Anxiety breeds these two problems – limitation and fear. A soul battling with these two evils cannot be happy. Anxiety is that culprit that steals your joy by preoccupying you with unnecessary agitation and worry. Happiness is the bedrock of any relationship, so stop being sad and start enjoying happy moments with your partner by taking the following steps:

- Dismiss any thoughts that make you sad

- Play your favorite music to occupy your mind

- Become playful with your partner

- Relive the sweet moments you have had with your partner

- Be humorous, laugh with your partner

## 6. Anxiety can either makes you distant or clingy

One way by which you can recognize anxious people is that they tend to be extreme in their actions. If they are not aloof, they will become too attached. Both of these behaviors are extreme and unhealthy. Have you evaluated yourself and discovered that you are guilty of these extremities? Take the action steps below to restore your healthy relationship with your partner:

- Figure out your feelings

- Work on yourself

- Get yourself engaged with things you enjoy doing

## 7. Anxiety makes you reject things that will benefit you.

It makes you see everything from one point of view - fear. Anxiety results in indecision in a relationship, because you won't know which way is right. Here is how you can stop this problem:

- Acknowledge your confusing thoughts and deal with them

- Weigh your decisions carefully without being biased

- Seek your partner's help if you discover you need support

## Practical Strategies to Solving Anxiety Issues in a Relationship

Partners/couples generally face challenges which need to be addressed as the partnership progresses. Your ability to manage issues as they come up in your relationship will ultimately determine the growth of the relationship. If a challenge is not well managed, you may find your relationship in a crisis and may need to take concrete steps towards charting a way out.

Some of the challenges that most people face in their relationships include communication, joint development as a couple, relationship needs, contentedness and autonomy of the partners, equal rights, routine, habit, sexuality, loyalty, stress, quarrels, conflicts, difference in value systems, distance, illness, and the list goes on.

How careful are you in your relationship? Being careful and considerate of each other saves a lot of frustration in the relationship. Do you live in the here and now? Can you enjoy the moment? Living in the here and now sounds easier than it is. More often than not, our thoughts slide into the past or the future.

Other questions to ask yourself about your relationship:

How intensely are you enjoying the moment? Does your partner always understand what you mean? Do you do a lot in common together? Are both of you a well-rehearsed team in all walks of life? Do you find security, tenderness and sexual satisfaction with your partner? How about division of labor - does it work well between the both of you? Do you find peace, support, and security in your relationship? Can you talk about everything very openly? Does your partner make you strong and happy?

The answers to these questions will guide you into a proper self-evaluation of the challenges you might be facing in your relationship.

In most cases, men do not like relationship talks. Nevertheless, it is necessary to exchange regularly about needs and wishes in a partnership. Especially for conflict resolution, communication strategies are needed. Firstly, you must distinguish between generally communicating as partners and communication as a result of conflict resolution. Communication about each partner's wishes, ideas, plans, and hopes is an important foundation for a relationship. Couples who are happy in long term relationships are usually able to communicate their feelings to each other, and they do not see themselves or their relationship threatened by these expressions, even if they are negative without being aware of it.

They are able to develop their own, very subtle language, gestures, and facial expressions throughout their relationship.

Quarrels are normal in a relationship - it is the "how" that matters. Clashes arise when you or your partner are strained by external stress. For example a job, problems in raising children, conflicts in the family, etc. The stressed partner often communicates in a more irritated and violent tone.

It is in our greatest interest to be proactive and inventive regarding how we communicate with those closest to us.

Creating, maintaining, and nurturing relationships with friends, co-workers, and family, not just partners, is critical for our well-being.

Rather than looking to others to create relationship changes, the simplest place to start out is with yourself.

## A Relationship Self-Assessment

Below is a list of some relationship statements. Go through the statements and make note of any that don't seem to be very true for you. Write these down on a separate sheet of paper.

1. I have told my spouse/partner/children, that I really like them within the previous few days or week.

2. I get on well with my siblings.

3. I get on well with my coworkers and/or clients.

4. I get on well with my manager and/or employees.

5. There is nobody I might dread or feel uncomfortable running across.

6. I place relationships first and results second.

7. I have forsaken all of the relationships that drag me down or injury me

8. I have communicated or tried to speak with

everybody I may have hurt, injured, or seriously disturbed, though it may not have been 100% my fault.

9. I don't gossip to or about others.

10. I have a circle of friends and/or family who I love and appreciate.

11. I tell people close to me that I appreciate them.

12. I am completely wrapped up in letters, emails, and calls relating to work.

13. I always tell the truth, even if it may hurt.

14. I receive enough love from people around me to feel appreciated.

15. I have forgiven those people that have hurt or broken me, whether or not it was deliberate.

16. I keep my word; people can rely on me.

17. I quickly clear up miscommunications and misunderstandings after they occur.

18.    I live life on my terms, not by the principles or preferences of others.

19. There is nothing unresolved with my past loves or spouses.

20.    I am in tune with my needs and desires and ensure they are taken care of.

21. I don't judge or criticize others.

22.    I have a supporter or lover.

23.    I talk openly about issues instead of grumbling.

Relationship Problem: Money

Many relationship problems start with money. Whether one person manages it differently than the other, or there has been mistrust due to mismanagement of finances in the past, money can strain even the strongest relationship.

Problem-solving strategies:

Be honest concerning your current monetary scenario. Don't approach the topic when the situation is tense. Rather, set aside a suitable and convenient time for both of you.

Acknowledge the fact that one of you will always be a spender while the other person is a saver, talk about the advantages of each, and try to learn from each other.

Do not keep your financial gain or debt away from your partner. If at some point you want to join finances, lay out all monetary documents including recent credit reports, pay stubs, bank statements, insurance policies, debts, and investments.

When things go wrong with finances, never apportion blame. Pieces of paper and ones and zeros on a computer are insignificant compared to your human connection.

When it comes to shared money, incorporate savings into a joint budget and decide that your payment of monthly bills is a joint responsibility. Still allow the both of you to be independent by putting aside some money to be spent when the need arises.

Make decisions concerning your long term as well as short term goals. It's normal to have personal goal, but you must not underestimate the importance of family goals.

Relationship Problem: Struggles Over Home Chores

A majority of partners work outside the house and sometimes at more than one job. Therefore, it is vital to fairly divide the household responsibilities.

Problem-solving strategies:

Be organized and clear regarding your jobs within the home. Write all the roles down and agree on who will do what, or what schedule to work off of. Be honest about what you do or do not want to do and what you have time for.

**Be open to alternative solutions:** If you each hate housework, perhaps you'll be able to spring for a cleaning service. Or maybe you can be a bit more lax about the level of cleanliness around the house. If you're a neat freak but your partner isn't, is there a compromise to be found? Always make an effort to meet in the middle.

Relationship Problem: Not prioritizing your relationship

If you wish to keep your relationship going, prioritizing your relationship is a must. Make it important and worth your while. Recognize the importance of it, cherish it, and nourish it so that it will stand the test of time.

Problem-solving strategies:

Go back to those things you did when you started dating. Appreciate one another, give compliments, contact one another through the day, and show genuine interest in each other.

Schedule a time to go on a date and plan it with as much consideration as when you were trying to win each other over.

Respect is very important. Learn to be appreciative. If you partner does something that makes you happy, never hesitate to show your gratitude by saying thank you. Let your partner know what matters most to you - them.

Relationship Problem: Conflict

Occasional conflict is a part of life. However, if you and your partner are constantly arguing, it is time to break the cycle and be freed from this poisonous routine. Instead of getting angry, look carefully into underlying problems and look for possible ways to solve the issue without hostility.

Problem-solving strategies:

You and your partner will learn to argue in an exceedingly civil, useful manner.

Realize you're not a victim - it's your choice if you react they way you do. Be honest with yourself and with your partner about how you feel.

Once you are in the middle of an argument, pay attention to how you phrase things and the tone of your voice. Would you be okay with your partner speaking to you the way you're speaking to them? Put love and kindness first, and never forget that the person you're arguing with is also the person you've chosen to spend your life with. Is the conflict worth more than the relationship?

If you still respond with the kind of approach that has brought you pain and unhappiness within the past, you cannot expect a different result at this point. For example, if you were in the habit of interrupting your partner before they are done talking because you want to defend yourself, hold off for some moments. You will be shocked at how such a change in tempo will have a remarkable effect on the tone of an argument.

Give a little, get heaps. Apologize when you are wrong. It's a powerful way to show your partner that you value them above being right. Try it and see the amazing result.

You cannot manage the behavior of another person; you must not fail to acknowledge the fact that you are only in charge of yourself.

Relationship Problem: Trust

Trust is vital as far as relationship is concerned. Are you always seeing things that make your trust for your partner dwindle? Or do you have issues that are not yet resolved and this is making you not trust other people?

Problem-solving strategies:

You and your partner will develop trust in one another by considering the following pointers.

- Always be consistent.

- Be on time.

- Never fail to do what you have promised to do.

- Don't tell a lie -- not even a white lie to your lover or any other person.

- Be fair, even in an argument.

- Be sensitive to the other's feelings. You'll still disagree, however do not discount how your partner is feeling.

- Call when you say you'll.

- Call to mention you will be home late.

- Carry your weight and fulfill promises and responsibilities.

- Never say things you cannot take back.

- Don't reopen old wounds.

- Have regard for your partner's boundaries.

- Avoid being needlessly jealous.

Always be realistic. Thinking your partner can meet all of your wants -- and will be able to figure them out without your saying anything -- might be closer to a Hollywood fantasy. Ask for what you would like directly.

You should be ever ready to make your relationship work and to really look into what must be done. Do not conclude that you can't enjoy a peaceful and loving relationship with another person until you have looked over all the conflicts and attempted to address them. Unless you attend to the issues in your current relationship, any future relationships will be marred by the same problems.

# Chapter 4: Identifying Behaviors that Trigger Anxiety

Unhealthy anxiety can have a big impact on your life. It will hinder you from doing the things you desire. When you are anxious, you get a feeling that your life is under the control of an external force. Anxiety is a negative, vicious circle which consumes you completely and can have an effect on your wellbeing, your relationship, your hobbies, and more. It feels difficult to break this anxiety, but the possibility exists. Anxiety often makes people assume that they are no longer in charge and cannot do anything about it. This isn't the case - you can learn to get your anxieties under control and find happiness.

Anxiety disorder occurs when you regularly feel disproportionate levels of worry, tension, or fear due to an emotional trigger. The ability to identify the reason behind a series of anxiety attacks is the key to successful treatment.

1. Environmental factors: Elements within your surroundings can trigger anxiety. Worries and stress associated with a private relationship, job, school, or monetary difficulty can lead to anxiety disorder.

2. Genetics: Research has shown that if any members of your family have dealt with anxiety disorder, there is high chance that you will experience anxiety as well.

3. Medical factors: Different medical issues can lead to an anxiety disorder, such as the side effects of drugs, symptoms of a sickness, or stress from a difficult underlying medical condition. These conditions could lead to significant lifestyle changes like pain, restricted movement, and even emotional imbalance. It is worth noting that anxiety can be triggered by any of these problems.

4. Brain chemistry: Experiences that are traumatising or stressful can alter the structure

and performance of the brain, making it react to certain triggers that may not have previously caused anxiety.

Relationships are amazing and very fulfilling with the opportunity for happiness, fun, interesting conversations, and exciting dates. They can, however, also be a major source of upheaval and worry. Your ability to identify the major sources of anxiety in your relationship will help you stay away from them, thus enhancing the balance and stability of your relationship.

I will now take you through some of the most common triggers of anxiety in your relationships and how to look out for them and control them.

What triggers anxiety the most is when you are vulnerable to another person. We yearn for safety and love in a relationship. If you have been hurt before, the fear of being hurt again can make you anxious.

Financial concerns of either partner is another cause of anxiety in relationships. Most times, people do not fully disclose their money related issues or financial strengths. They open up when a problem arises, and at this point it may be too late. It could be that you are not compatible with your partner when it comes to saving and spending money, or you do not even share the same money views with them. It is also easy for you to get carried away by love and close your eyes to the financial wherewithal of your partner. When real life expenses sets in and you seem to be carrying the brunt of them, anxiety sets in. Money in relationships is a constant.

Another root cause of anxiety in relationships is jealousy. Your inability to trust your partner could lead to jealousy. Jealousy is also as a result of a lack of confidence in yourself and your abilities coupled with low self-esteem. In order to overcome this, build up your self-esteem and begin to think very highly of yourself. The best way to eradicate jealousy is by building up your self-esteem.

Jealousy can reveal our greatest fears and insecurities, and this can quickly lead to an unhealthy and toxic atmosphere in your relationship. When you are jealous, you become overwhelmed and begin to imagine the worst.

The fear of being abandoned and the fear of rejection are also major causes of anxiety in relationships. Whatever insecurities you have are mirrored back to you by your partner. It is only normal to worry about these things, but instead of keeping the thoughts to yourself, speak them out loud and have a conversation about them with your partner. You have to develop a stronger identity and sense of self. You have to learn to be consciously aware of your state of mind and thought processes in order to keep all anxieties at bay. Most of the arguments you have with your partner over your family, work, social life, or money actually have some form of rejection as their roots. The underlying feeling and fear during these fights is that you will be rejected. For instance, if you are having a heated discussion about how much time your partner spends with his friends, it is actually about why they aren't spending that time with you?

Your ability to relax into your relationship will make you feel less rejected and no longer defensive. Be present in your relationship and have no negative thoughts.

You must deliberately set clear boundaries on the type of information that gets into your head. Work to stop unwanted information and behaviors from coming in and penetrating into your mind.

When anxiety comes knocking at your door, open the door for it, address it, look at it, then inhale deeply and close the door, knowing that you have armed yourself with all the information that you need. You do not have to welcome anxiety with open arms, but you can acknowledge that it's there.

Ongoing communication with an ex is another trigger for anxiety. Communications with an ex should be handled cautiously. This is because it can lead to great anxiety, anger, and eventually a breakup in your current relationship. If you have to communicate with your ex, you should explain why to your partner and ensure all communication is strictly platonic and transparent. If you do not have to communicate with your ex, do not do it.

Distance backed up with a lack of communication can hugely contribute to anxiety between you and your partner. When your partner is not physically available for a long period of time, it can be difficult to find assurance and thus anxiety sets in. Even if you talk on the phone and video call regularly, you can still feel a void in your heart. In situations like this, you have to rely on the power of words to communicate your feelings with your partner. Feel free to tell your partner what you need from them, express yourself, and talk about any insecurities you may be going through. By so doing, your partner will be able to address this and reassure you of their love and commitment.

Another major cause of anxiety is doubt. It can be weakening to question every move and action of your partner, wondering if you made the right decision or what next steps you should or should not take. If you are in great doubt, begin to make a conscious effort to release yourself and set yourself free from doubt. Take your mind off every question that makes you doubt your relationship or your partner. Just take a deep breathe, calm down, and revel in your relationship. Make up your mind to just enjoy your relationship and your partner by allowing yourself the freedom of not having to make any decisions about your relationship for a period of time.

A major health challenge can also trigger anxiety in your relationship. You or your partner may be caught off guard by a diagnosis or medical scare. This may also stress you out and cause a great deal of anxiety within yourself. If you or your partner fall ill, anxiety will naturally set in. This health challenge may cause your partner to break down emotionally. You will have to be very patient and calm with them through this process. Provide all the support you can during this time and let them be assured of your unwavering love and commitment.

## How to Put a Stop to these Behaviors

Anxiety not only stresses you, it can also cause distress in your relationship as a whole. Being in a relationship with an anxious partner can be confusing, and you must take steps to address to the triggers of anxiety in your relationship.

You should also note that the quality and experiences in a relationship can also lead to anxiety. It may not necessarily be about your attitude or your partner's behavior. As the relationship progresses, things can get complicated, and controlling anxiety in your relationship has more to do with you first than with your partner.

A major way to put a stop to anxiety and its triggers in your relationship is to exercise and practice other anxiety reduction strategies. You can easily integrate exercise into your daily life immediately. Research has proven that exercise is as powerful as most anxiety medications for putting a stop to anxiety symptoms.

You can also try to rebuild the trust in your relationship as a way to clear all anxiety that may exist. If you feel the trust in your relationship is gone, have a conversation with your partner about starting the relationship all over again from the beginning. Trust is the foundation of a relationship, and it needs to grow and be healthy. Give yourself and your partner some time to cultivate a loving and trusting relationship again.

Communication about your needs is also important to quenching all anxieties in your relationship. Talk about your needs with your partner; write them down so no one forgets. Then be sure to also address your partner's needs and wants, which are just as important as your own.

Another way to put a stop to anxious behaviors is to be mentally busy. When you fill up your mind with other productive activities, you are able to get your mind off your relationship. This decreases the frequency with which your mind can wander into negative emotions. Activities such as reading an engaging book, hanging out with friends, going on dates, watching TV, and doing other outdoor activities can improve the mood of your relationship and help you stay mentally busy.

As much as possible, be very physical with your partner during anxious moments. Touching, holding of hands, and kissing even when you are mad at your partner is very important. Remaining affectionate even in stressful or difficult times helps you both to reconnect and be reassured that the love and intimacy have not gone out the window.

You will need to keep trying, learn to calm yourself, reassure yourself, and comfort yourself in anxious situations. Make up your mind to have a healthy mind and manage stress and negativity in your life.

You can also practice deep breathing exercises. These are relaxation techniques which can help you manage panic issues, reduce stress, and bring about calm.

When you breathe deeply, your focus will be on the breathing process, which involves your belly and rib cage being completely filled with each inhalation, followed by complete exhalations, thereby letting all of the air out. These easy to learn breathing exercises reduce anxiety drastically. You will feel more relaxed, energized, and refreshed. When you take fuller breaths, you feel calmer and more in control when anxiety comes knocking. It helps you to shift your focus towards the rhythm of your breath and clears your mind of anxious, fearful, and negative thoughts.

All relationships need trust, tenderness, patience, and a touch of vulnerability. Individuals with anxiety usually have these by the truckload and can provide them liberally to the connection. The problem is that anxiety works to erode some of these qualities while amplifying others.

All relationships experience struggles, but once anxiety is at play, the struggles become further ingrained and more difficult to manage.

Here are some ways in which you can strengthen your relationship and defend it from the impact of anxiety:

**Top up the emotional resources.**

The emotional connection between you and your partner is what we are talking about here. What anxiety does is to drain and weaken the emotional connection between the two of your. Top up your emotional resources by being sensitive to both the physical and emotional needs of your partner.

**Let your partner see you as a support, too.**

Your partner may feel reluctant to 'burden' you with worries, notably if those worries don't appear as massive as the ones you're battling.

People with anxiety have a great deal of strength. Be sure to let your partner know that it doesn't matter however massive or little their struggles are - you're there to support and help them, too. The tendency will be for partners of anxious individuals to dismiss their own worries, however this may mean that they are doing themselves out of the chance to feel nurtured and supported by you – which might be a large loss for each of you.

### Let your partner in on what you're thinking

Anxious thoughts are supremely personal, but it's beneficial to let your partner in on them. It's a vital a part of intimacy, and the essence of a relationship is intimacy. You are acting contrary to this purpose anytime you fail to share whatever is bothering you with your partner. Apart from that, it has also been discovered that couples who do not share their thoughts with each other are emotionally detached. So, let your partner know what you are thinking. It does not only strengthen the bond, but you are also relieved from the burden of whatever occupies your mind.

### Asking for support is completely okay – but there are limits

Anxiety injects a feeling of unpleasantness into everything. Once it's left ungoverned, it can cause you to doubt the things that should not be doubted – like your relationship. It's more than okay and is in fact healthy to turn to your partner for support. An excessive amount of it, however, might be felt as neediness. Neediness is the enemy of a healthy relationship and over time will smother the spark.

### It's normal to feel vulnerable

Uneasiness can impact the connection between you and your partner in diverse ways. In some individuals, it may trigger the tendency for consistent consolation while in others, it can make them give in to despair. Vulnerability – being emotionally available to others - is delightful and is the quintessence of effective, solid connection. Vulnerability is normal, and you shouldn't shy away from it or let its presence make you feel anxious.

### Uncomfortable discussions can bring you closer

Don't avoid painful topics just because they make you uncomfortable or you're afraid they will cause trouble. All relationships will have "uncomfortable" topics that are unique to the couple, but shying away from them can make it worse. The temptation may be to abstain from discussing troublesome issues with your partner in light of worries about what they may do the relationship. Troublesome issues don't leave – they get worse until they reach a breaking point. Trust that your partner – and yourself – can handle difficult discussions. Connections are based on trust, and believing that your relationship can go through troublesome discussions and come out unscathed is significant.

### Tell your partner what triggers you

Is there a specific circumstance that will in general set your nervousness or anxiety in motion? Groups? Outsiders? Change of plans? Loud music in the vehicle? Being late? Talk to your partner about all of these things so that on the off chance that you end up in these circumstances, they will recognize that you're going through something and will be able to help you or put a stop to whatever is triggering your anxiety.

*Ensure you're taking care of yourself*

Being infatuated is a lovely and overpowering feeling - however, it can lead to you pouring all your attention into your partner and neglecting yourself. This is especially troublesome for someone with anxiety. Remembering to eat well, exercise, and take time out for yourself will not only keep you healthy physically, your mental health will be impacted as well. On the off chance that taking care of yourself feels egotistical, consider it along these lines: if you don't take care of yourself, how can you take care of your partner?

Consider self-care as an interest in you, your relationship, and your partner. Keep in mind too that anything that is useful for combating anxiety is useful for everybody, so converse with your partner about pursuing a sound way of life together – cooking, exercising, and making time for self-care.

*Understand that your partner will have limitations*

You should be conscious of the fact that your partner

is human, and therefore they have their limitations. So, you should not expect them to be perfect at all times. You will save yourself from unnecessary anxiety when you are conscious of this fact. Realize that nagging or dwelling extensively over an issue will not benefit your relationship. Communication is important in a relationship, but when you keep talking over and over again about the same issue without seeking a resolution, it can be very frustrating. So, you need to take note of this.

Also, you should acknowledge the fact that your partner loves you and cherishes you. Your ability to accept the limitations of your partner will help you overcome anxiety issues. Welcome their limitations – this action will strengthen your relationship and foster love. Stress is an enemy of relationships. Mutual understanding of each other's weakness eliminates stress in a relationship. However, stress strives if partners refuse to accept each other the way they are.

### Laugh together

This is so significant! Laughing is a natural cure to the pressure and strain that accompanies relationships. Finding humor in life will bring you closer together, especially in times of distress, and help you remember why you fell in love in the first place. Anxiety has a way of making you forget that life isn't supposed to be taken so seriously. If you haven't laughed in a while, find something that will make you smile, to begin with. A funny movie, something on YouTube, memories of the past...anything.

The starry eyed beginning of love is as enchanting as it is short lived. Relationships, no matter how good, come with their highs and lows. From the delight of realizing that someone loves you as much as you love them, to the desolation of uncertainty, to the security of knowing that you're in it for the long haul - every partnership will see both times of joy and times of sorrow. Anxiety can prolong these sorrows - if you let it. By purposefully working to form a solid connection with your partner, you can stop anxious behaviors in their tracks.

## A Deep Breathing Exercise

When practicing the following deep breathing exercise, you need to be in a quiet environment before you move on to the steps:

Begin by sitting upright in a chair or on the floor in any comfortable position, such as on your back.

Keep your eyes shut in order to reflect inward and focus.

Begin to be aware of your breath. Are you breathing slowly, or very fast?

Now begin to breathe intentionally, making sure to keep your shoulders relaxed and still. Inhale in deeply and slowly through your nose. You will feel your diaphragm expand as you are able to fill your body with air. Now you can begin to slowly exhale out through your mouth, allowing the stale air to leave your body.

Continue to focus on your breath; repeat 5-10 more cycles of deep breathing.

The moment you begin to breathe deeply, you will begin to notice that some areas of your body feel less tense than other areas. This is because your body releases stress with each exhale.

Before you conclude this exercise, notice how you feel physically, mentally, and emotionally.

In order to get the most out of this exercise, it is important that you practice regularly and at times when you do not even feel anxious.

Another strategy to help you cope with anxiety is progressive muscle relaxation. This is an exercise that you can use to reduce disturbing bouts of anxiety. It is a type of relaxation technique, and it can help you in moments of high stress or during panic attack. By relaxing your body, you will be able to let go of anxious thoughts and feelings.

## Progressive Muscle Relaxation: Step-by-Step Techniques

Stay in a comfortable position - you can either sit down or lie down. Eliminate all distractions and close your eyes for improved concentration.

Through your nose, breathe deeply. You will feel your abdomen rise as your body fills up with air. Slowly exhale from your mouth, drawing your navel toward your spine. Repeat this process 3-5 times.

Tighten your feet and release your muscles, clench your toes and press your heels towards the ground. Squeeze tightly for a few breaths, and then release.

Continue to tighten and release each muscle group. Your legs, hands, arms, shoulders, neck, face. Tighten each muscle group for a few breaths and then slowly release.

Bring the practice to an end by taking a few more breaths. You will notice that you feel more calm and relaxed.

## How to Stop Worrying So Much

When you are dealing with anxiety or a panic disorder, worry is also commonplace. You get worried about your partner, the state of your relationship, your finances, the future - the list is endless. You may find yourself worrying about things that haven't even happened or are out of your control, such as the health, safety, and security of your relationship and a whole lot of other issues which constantly drain you.

When you worry so much, it becomes a heavy burden and affects your relationship negatively. It also affects your personality, self-esteem, career, and other aspects of your life. You may even find yourself breaking down emotionally and mentally. It is important to know how to put worry at bay. Worry does not have to control your life, and you can reduce it by practicing the following steps:

Set aside some amount of time for worrying. It may seem counterintuitive to schedule "worry time," but this may be just what you need to reduce your anxious thoughts.

You can begin by determining what time of the day you wish to put aside to worry. It could be in the morning, so that you can get worry over and done with, or at night so you can let go of it before you sleep. This can help to clear your mind of all the worries that build up throughout the day.

Talk to others about worrying. You may find some relief by sharing your thoughts and feelings with a trusted friend or family member. Family members can be a great source of support; they can provide you with the needed love, support, and guidance you will need throughout this period.

You can also keep a journal to help you work through worry and anxiety. If you feel like you do not have anyone to talk to, a journal may be all you need to work through your inner mind, feelings, emotions, and worries.

By learning the act of positive thinking, you may be able to totally put a stop to worrying. Worry is a negative thinking pattern and can contribute to your anxiety and panic disorder. Turn your thoughts around by taking a look at the other side of worry or a negative thought. Replace those negative thoughts with more realistic and positive statements.

You should also learn to relax your mind and body in order to conquer anxiety. When you are in a relaxed state, it's harder to feel worried. You can practice different activities to take your mind off worries and help you stay relaxed.

## Ways to Work through Worry

You won't always be able to just stop worrying, but you can learn how to manipulate the feeling so that it does not take over or interfere with your life. Sometimes, the best way to control worry is to acknowledge it, then take steps to work through it.

### Get More Sleep

Just like after a night of overindulging, sometimes

you just need to sleep it off. Worry and anxiety are more apt to take hold if you are mentally and physically exhausted. By getting enough sleep, you're taking steps to solve the problem before it even starts. While worry and anxiety can keep us up at night and even wake us up from our peaceful slumber, take advantage of the restful nights or nap during the day to keep your energy levels up and raise your ability to push back worry. This has the added benefit of making you less irritable, more healthy, and more focused in your personal life and at work. This in turn takes away some of the causes of worry, such as poor health or poor work performance.

### Recognize the Root of Worry

When you're worrying about something, do you even know why? Often, our train of thought runs so quickly that what we are consciously worrying about may not be what originally triggered the reaction to begin with. Follow your thoughts backward to discover where the worry came from. If you only pay attention to what's at the forefront of your mind, you'll ignore the vast resource that is your subconscious.

For example, let's say you're struck with the worrying thought that your partner might be thinking about ending things. You'll think over the various signs, whether real or imagined, and begin to slide down the embankment of fear and irrationality. But wait! Why did the thought occur in the first place? Why are you worrying about something that may not even be true? Maybe you feel that there has been a lack of intimacy lately, or your partner isn't giving you the attention you desire. Instead of giving in to worry and thinking up the worse case scenario, follow the thought back and determine what the real reason for your worry is so that you can take action.

### Write it Down

Journaling is, as mentioned, very useful when dealing with anxiety. If you find that your thoughts are overwhelming and you can't concentrate on anything, empty your mind by putting everything in it on paper. Sometimes, seeing your fears written out helps you to see how insignificant or irrational they are. Even if that's not the case, you'll have a hard copy to refer to instead of a fleeting wisp of a thought that comes out of nowhere at the most inconvenient time.

### Follow the Train of Thought

It might seem counterproductive to focus on what you're worrying about, but it can sometimes help to play out your fears in your mind and discover that the catastrophic end result you imagine might not be that bad after all. When you start to worry, follow wherever your thoughts go.

If you start to worry that your partner is bored with you, play out the consequences in your mind. If they're bored with me, they'll look for someone else. If they look for someone else, they'll succeed in no time because they're great. They'll either leave me for this person or cheat on me. What next?

Once you get to the end of the thought process, you can examine the chain of events to determine how likely they are, or you can take steps to prevent them from happening. For example, you can go back to the first thought of "they're bored with me" and decide to spice things up. Whether the reality is that they're bored or not doesn't matter. If you can acknowledge your fears and worries and take steps to address them, you'll remove the cause and thus the symptom.

### Pick Something You Can Control

As with the previous example, if your worrying thoughts include something that you can act on, by all means do it! Much of your anxiety and worry come from places of fear that tell you the unknown is scary and uncomfortable, thus you need to try to control it so that you know what to expect. While you'll never be able to know everything, you can take steps to prepare for what might come. You don't need to control your destiny - only the present, and only within your own life. Take back a feeling of control by exerting your influence, however small.

# Chapter 5: Conflicts in Relationships

Conflicts arise in relationships from time to time. It could be due to financial problems, your families who interfere in your decisions, your professional career, the education of your children, or your new life with the addition of a baby. All of these elements and more are the source of arguments between you and your partner and can lead to conflicts in the relationship. When this happens from time to time, do not worry too much, because arguments can sometimes be for the good for the relationship.

Nevertheless, you must learn not to let negative situations last too long, otherwise your relationship may be greatly weakened. Indeed, conflicts in your relationship are synonymous with the first step that destabilizes a relationship. You therefore need to be able to manage these situations well to find serenity, complicity, and thus revive the flame. To make sure your relationship can continue or even get off to a good start, you should never let things get worse by standing idly by or thinking it will be better tomorrow.

Love is not a given - you have to constantly work on yourself and your relationship. If you do not act in time and allow a conflict to persist in your relationship, you risk getting dangerously close to separation.

## What are the reasons for conflict between couples?

In order to face the monster in your relationship and face your fears, the first step is to understand the origin of the conflict between yourself and your partner and to fix it properly.

Indeed, you will not be able to completely adjust the tensions in your relationship if you do not put your finger on the exact origin of the issue. In order to solve a problem effectively, you must know its roots. Otherwise, all you can do is put a band-aid on the problem. Small tensions can trigger big fights when issues remain unsolved.

The first thing to do to overcome conflicts in your relationship is to identify and acknowledge them.

As I mentioned in my introduction, there are many reasons for the situation your relationship is going through today. I will go over some of these reasons.

### Conflicts caused by professional life

Tensions can arise because you care more about your career than your partner - or at least, one of you may think so. This situation can make your partner or yourself react strongly. There is nothing worse than feeling abandoned by someone you love.

Focusing more on your professional life than your personal life is not only unhealthy when you're single, it is detrimental when you're in a relationship.

It is sometimes really difficult to reconcile work and family, especially when you want to start a business or have a very stressful job. But, to have a balanced life and to avoid conflicts in your relationship, it is imperative to learn to disconnect from work and to enjoy life with your loved ones.

### Infidelity and Inappropriate Behavior

There are attitudes to ban when you are in a relationship. If you stick to a behavior that your partner considers to be unforgivable, you will have trouble picking up the pieces and inevitably your relationship will experience periods of turbulence.

There may also be conflicts between couples in the case of infidelity. If you are in this situation, you'll be dealing with struggles beyond the scope of this book. Seek out therapy, whether for yourself or for you both.

### When Your Partner No Longer Meets Your Expectation

Life evolves, grows, and changes. Relationships do, as well. Sometimes, two people in a relationship grow separately and reach a point where they are no longer the people they were when they began the relationship.

When this happens, sit down and have a conversation about it. What expectations do either of you have that aren't being met? Are these expectations reasonable? The only way to gauge where the relationship is to talk about it.

To overcome the conflicts in your love life, whatever the source of the tensions are, the first thing that you must seek to understand is why the conflicts are there to begin with. To do this, talk to your partner. The discussion may be uncomfortable, but it is necessary. Your anxiety might be heightened, but don't let if force you into rash behaviors. Calm discussions do more for conflicts than anxiety-fuelled arguments.

Many couples try to avoid fighting as much as possible. Others will blame the other person for being the cause of arguments. These reactions don't resolve struggles and may even exacerbate issues.

Struggle are an ordinary part of life and

relationships. When ignored, they cause more harm. When faced head on, they become the tools to help couples grow closer by solving conflicts together.

Struggles can emerge from mistaken assumptions about:

- The nature of the relationship

- Varying assumptions regarding how things ought to be done around the house

- Work

- The various obligations of each partner

- Contrasts in morals, values, needs, or wants

- Poor communication

## What Conflicts do to Anxiety

When problems crop up in a relationship, you might feel like all of your anxieties are warranted and finally proving to be true. Don't give in to this way of thinking! Anxiety stems from the unknown, and conflicts arise when expectations are not met or differences in opinion to light. They are healthy when handled properly, while anxiety is nothing but detrimental. Some of the ways conflict might affect anxiety include:

## *Increased Heart Rate*

Conflict can cause a release of adrenaline, which anxiety only makes worse. This can lead to rapid heart beat which in turn causes shortness of breath and increased anxiety thanks to these physiological symptoms. It's a vicious cycle. The best way to combat this is to approach conflict with calmness. If you avoid raising your voice, becoming upset, or reacting in anger, you won't trigger an adrenaline release and thus will quel the feelings of anxiety.

## *Nervous Energy or Movement*

Again, thanks to adrenaline, your entire body will react by suddenly filling with energy that has to be used in some way. Since during an argument you most likely won't be running or fighting, that energy translates into pacing, toe tapping, hand wringing, and general nervous movement and energetic tics. These can be uncomfortable for you and distracting to your partner when you're in the middle of a conflict. Of course, it's not your fault, but that knowledge doesn't make it go away. As above, approach the situation with calm rather than anxiety to prevent the release of adrenaline.

### Panic and Anxiety Attacks

Anxiety can lead to anxiety attacks? How shocking.

This might not be new information, but it's beneficial to your health to remember that in conflicts, it's in your best interest to keep calm if you have difficulties with anxiety and panic. The situation can trigger an attack, which can make everything worse. Panic and anxiety attacks are typically characterized by:

- shortness of breath

- difficulty focusing

- sweating

- racing thoughts

- feeling of impending doom

Needless to say, these are not fun symptoms, and it pays to be mindful before entering into an argument that if you don't remain level headed, you could stir up an attack.

### Defensive Behavior

Nothing is more detrimental to constructive conflict resolution than defensiveness. Anxiety can block the more rational part of your mind that can think through a situation logically. Without this logic, you may have a hard time concentrating on what your partner is saying an, instead of listening, cause you to lash out and go on the defense, even if your partner is not attacking you. While you should absolutely defend yourself when unjustly treated, if your partner is seeking a peaceful resolution the best course of action is to match their intentions and drop the defensiveness. Of course, when you have anxiety, that's not so easy.

118

### Shut Down

Instead of becoming defensive, you might just shut down entirely. The anxious mind may be unable to process what is happening and lack the energy to work through the situation, leading to a total shut down. When this happens, you are unable to focus or concentrate, you can't call on logic or rationality to work through a conflict, and you may even be unable to comprehend what your partner is saying. On the inside, you will feel heavy and empty, like you are a battery that was suddenly drained. The best thing to do when this happens is to rest and recuperate. Conflicts will keep until you're able to take back your mind and put your rationality in charge.

## The Key to Overcoming a Bad Dispute in a Relationship

When faced with a conflict in your relationship that is growing, think about the way you express your feelings or talk about this conflict with your partner. Good communication is where everyone can take stock and try to understand the attitude of the other.

The conflict will be easier to manage when it's not exacerbated by angry tones and unnecessary insults.

For effective conflict communication, there are 3 rules to follow:

- Avoid raising your voice and keep calm whenever a conflict happens.

- Allow your partner to talk and develop their argument, because communication not only involves talking, but also listening.

- Find a middle ground, but do not make compromises that can have negative consequences in the future.

A couple who argues but who respects these three rules will find it easier to come to a resolution.

### Actions needed to overcome conflict between couples

Relationships are not always easy, and you are constantly learning. Is it possible not to repeat the same mistakes and stabilize one's romantic relationship? How can you manage conflicts in your relationships without becoming a doormat?

Follow these recommendations to rebuild the love in a struggling relationship:

- Once you understand the reasons for the tensions that are shaking your relationship, you can move on to the more "direct" phase of reconciliation. It is true that the first step can be very psychological, because you have to communicate with your partner.

- It is necessary to put in place more technical and thoughtful actions to find the heart of your partner and to overcome the crisis of your relationship.

- The actions you have decided to put in place must correspond to the different issues, otherwise the latter will not have any particular effects and may perhaps even aggravate the situation. Don't seek resolution just to be done with it - seek resolution to make it better.

- Don't assign blame on either side. Relationships are a team effort, and both of you need to be in it fully, or not at all.

- If your partner or yourself are not feeling fulfilled in your relationship, you need to spend time together to better understand your issues and what both of you need from the relationship.

Every relationship experiences conflict at one point or the other. It is important to know that disagreement is not necessarily a bad thing - it is a way by which people express their diverse views on a situation or topic.

### Conflict Resolution in Healthy Relationships

Communication is the fuel that sustain a relationship. And, when we a say a relationship is healthy, it means the partners values communication and they never allow lack of communication to affect their togetherness. A good way to develop a healthy relationship is to practice successful conflict resolution without the interference of a third party.

It is normal to disagree on some matters; however, constant conflict is a sign of an unhealthy relationship. Therefore, if you argue with your partner on trivial issues like the kinds of friend you hang out with, where to go for dinner or date night, and who should take care of which household chores, then these tips are for you. They will help you resolve all your arguments amicably.

Do not cross your boundaries: Treat everyone with the respect they deserve, whether or not you are angry. Don't respond in kind if you partner ridicules you, calls you names, and uses provocative words during argument. Rather than replying to them, try to be calm and walk away if they are not yielding to your plea to stop. Let them know that you can proceed with the argument when tensions are lower.

Find out the root of the matter: Argument does not just happen; there must be a reason for it. So, an effective way to get a conflict solved is by unmasking the real issue. Try to understand your partner. Maybe they might need special attention, or they are just feeling insecure. Knowing the primary cause of an argument will help you to get it solved amicably. The summary of the point that I am trying to make here is that you should not shy away from the real issue.

Always resolve conflicts: It is always in your best interest to resolve every issue that comes up. Never pretend that all is well while you have something building inside you. Your goal is to have a healthy relationship, so everything needs to be out in the open. It is true that you cannot always be on the same page, but you must respect each other's differences.

Compromise when necessary: Compromise is one of the ingredients of a healthy relationship. You don't have to be dead set on winning the argument every time. There are some situations you just have to let go of and accept that you are wrong.

Take note of everything: You must not be indifferent to your partner. You should take time to consider the things that upset them, and also consider if you are taking advantage of them or being considerate enough. From which angle does your partner view issues? You need to find answers to these and many more questions, as they will help you better understand your partner.

If you have tried all the tricks above and the arguments persist, you should now look into the area of compatibility. Are you compatible with each other? If the answer is yes, then learn to work with each other and implement all you have learn from this book.

Conflict is a way of expressing your individual differences, but it should not degenerate into physical attacks or raining abuses on each other. This is never acceptable and is in fact the opposite of a healthy relationship. Never allow verbal abuse on either side, and know when to put an end to an argument if you discover that it is going in that direction.

Have in the back of your mind the knowledge that one of the signs of an unhealthy relationship is when a partner has a domineering attitude, and when a partner tries to manipulate or control the other at all times.

On a final note, pay attention to what upsets your partner. Here are some of the things that may annoy your partner:

- You are always making excuses not to do things with them (and maybe ask yourself why you do this)

- Rather than spending time with your partner, you went out with friends (do you spend an equal amount of time with your partner and your friends?)

- Not giving them your attention when they speak

- You don't reply their text or call after a reasonable amount of time

How to solve conflicts in your relationships by anticipation

Successfully defeating a conflict in a relationship is a good thing, and everything may feel rosy for a while. Of course, another issue will arise, but you should not allow these crises to recur too regularly, because constant conflict can lead to separation in the long term. Disputes can take on a life of their own, and turn into arguments that threaten the relationship.

You should therefore be prepared to anticipate these problems and do what you can to make your partner (and yourself) happy, not only during crises but also in everyday life. To do this, give your all in the relationship without waiting for the tensions to begin. Do not wait for the arguments - anticipate them and work to resolve them before they blow up, and you will see that your partner will act in exactly the same way.

# Chapter 6: Strategies to Improve Existing Relationships

If you've found someone you want to spend the foreseeable future with and would like to either start off on the right foot or work to improve the connection your already have, consider some of the following points:

## 1. Have common visions and values

If one person is a spendthrift and the other is thrifty, if one is watching their diet and the other eats only junk food, if one is on the right and the other on the left of the political spectrum, etc., chances are high that battles will take place - frequently.

For your relationship to last, you must have a set of commonalities for which you come together and a vision that allows you to project yourselves into a bright future.

All of this helps to share dreams and a good understanding of each other!

## 2. Gratify the other and give recognition

Whether you're married or not, much of what destroys couples and relationships comes from taking each other for granted. How does this translate into daily life?

When you refrain from putting in effort, when you do not do your part to nurture the relationship, when you criticize too much and too often, when you don't take their feelings to heart or acknowledge their struggles, and when you naively believe that your partner will love you forever, regardless of what you do.

Relationships do not work like that.

For each person in a relationship to feel loved and appreciated, both must express gratitude and recognition for the other on a regular basis.

This attitude nurtures collaboration, encourages a strong connection, and helps us appreciate our partner. They do not owe us their affection, so knowing that it is freely given is gratifying.

## 3. Be proud of the person with whom you are in a relationship

How can you live happily as a couple if you do not admire, at the very least, the person you are with?

There's no need to have received a Nobel Prize, cured cancer, or solved world hunger. If you do not appreciate at least one trait of the other person (intelligence, beauty, determination, courage, humor), you do not appreciate their place in your life. People gravitate towards those who express love, acceptance, and fulfillment. Make your partner feel loved and accepted all the time.

## 4. Have realistic expectations

Some women are continually looking for an impossible Prince Charming and believe that love must resemble a fairy tale, while men may be influenced by the unreasonable standards set by the media.

Whatever these unfounded expectations are, if they are unrealistic, by definition, they will generate disappointment.

Research into positive psychology has shown that it is better to have realistic and modest expectations as much as possible, even in your relationships.

If you are happy with what you have, you will find satisfaction.

If you are always looking to replace your partner with someone "better," without seeing their true qualities, you will condemn yourself to an eternal search for an illusion that exists only in your imagination.

## 5. Give affection a lot, and on a regular basis

Research has also shown that long-lasting couples are those who have been able to gradually replace love and passion with attachment.

We are not aware of it, but a lot of our behavior is determined by our hormones and our neurotransmitters. Cuddling, affection, and tenderness stimulate the production of oxytocin, the hormone of attachment.

If you want to feed the well-being of your partner, you must not forget the power of showing affection.

## 6. Do not let the sexual flame go out

After the passion at the beginning of your relationship, as time goes on, the frequency at which you make love might reduce. This can be for many reasons, none of which should be used to assign blame.

If this tendency continues, the sexual desire may end up being extinguished. Without (necessarily) bringing out the whip and the handcuffs, it is possible to continue to spark the sexual flame.

Yes, some clothes and toys can help, but the real key is to devote enough time to intimacy in your relationship, despite the tumult of everyday life.

Eating well, exercising, and staying healthy can help keep the flame alive despite the passage of time.

But, it also depends on your taste and your partner's. This fits into a more general vision which also comes from your own personal development and health.

## 7. Be open to improving and working on yourself.

If you or your partner constantly live in a state of pride and self-denial, it is clear that the relationship is preparing for doom.

Being in a partnership or relationship means working on yourself, making compromises, acknowledging shortcomings and mistakes, and working to correct them.

Proud people usually avoid this subject carefully: themselves, and more particularly their mistakes and faults. It will be difficult for you to live with such a person, unless you dream of sharing your life with a manipulator.

## 8. Stay faithful

To be faithful implies getting out of the excessive egotism that makes us prioritize our pleasure while ignoring that of the person we love.

A minimally empathetic person will quickly realize that if they would not want the other person to cheat on them, it is not acceptable behavior for themselves either.

If you claim to really love the other person, deceiving them becomes the last thing on your mind.

Love is one of the richest experiences we have to live through happiness and hardship. Why sully that with lies and unfaithfulness?

In short, romantic relationships are dynamic, like life, like those who live them. To live these enriching relationships, you must first come to recognize that your point of view is not the only point of view.

Only by trying to understand others do you come to build more fruitful relationships.

Respect, empathy and communication lead to more satisfying partnerships than the need to constantly be right.

Conflicts cannot be avoided in relationships. Two people who bring different life experiences to the table will inevitably have disagreements.

But when you strive to achieve your goals regardless of what the other person wants, you engage in behaviors that can only lead to a break-up. The challenge may be to bring different motivations together through common values, but you have a big tool to meet this challenge: communication.

To share your life with another person, basic wisdom requires you to make some sacrifices. When you do not communicate with your partner, even if the goal is to avoid conflict at all costs, you will only achieve even more disastrous results.

Regardless of whether you've been dating your partner for a short or long period of time, strong connections are formed when you accept the responsibility of making an effort and considering your partner's point of view.

While each relationship is unique, no relationship is impeccable. By doing these 9 things to improve your bond, you won't just guarantee a quality connection with your partner, you'll also demonstrate that you're resolved to work for one.

## 1. Ask your partner something new

Communication is the measure of togetherness in a relationship. It's pleasant to ask how your partner's day went, yet it's exhausting when you ask again and again. Communication must not be boring or redundant, so it your joint responsibility to keep yourself engaged with dialogues that are engaging and meaningful at the same time.

## 2. Assign a month to month night out on the town

Despite your busy schedules, ensure that you plan a night when the two of you will spend time together. Be consistent and be devoted to it once you have agreed on a date with your partner. If you're hoping to zest up your relationship or want to try something other than Netflix, leaving the house is a far more promising endeavor. More memories are made out in the world than on your couch.

## 3. Express your appreciation

The solace that a relationship offers is the reason we will, in general, ignore what our partner does and treat their demonstrations of affection as mandatory. To put it truly, your partner doesn't need to fill your gas tank or purchase your preferred frozen yogurt — they decide to because they love you, and your recognition and appreciation of the gesture will strengthen your relationship and inspire your partner to continue to be attentive and make you feel appreciated.

## 4. Change your timetable

We know — you're autonomous and don't anticipate ceasing your life for anybody (and you shouldn't need to). Despite the fact that you have different responsibilities outside of your relationship, it's a nice thought to check your calendars and see if there are conflicts preventing you from spending time together.

Maybe your partner can go to the gym earlier so you can make the late showing of a movie, or perhaps you can wake up earlier to complete your activities so you can make it to your partner's intramural game. While you shouldn't need to forfeit your life to fulfill your partner's, your capacity to bargain ought to be sufficient to satisfy that person.

## 5. Keep in mind the little things

Another approach to add importance to your discussion is to genuinely tune in to what your loved one is saying — and talk about it later on. If you need to, make note of something you talked about that you want to remember, or an event your partner mentioned that you want to follow up on. It's often the little things in conversations and relationships that make the biggest difference.

Also keep in mind the everyday things that, while small, can contribute to the happiness of your relationship. Reminders that you love the other person, have listened to them, or are thinking about them all seem like small gestures, but they are powerful.

## 6. Demonstrate your love

Apart from appreciating your partner, you need to let them know the extent of your love for them. You express your love through different gestures, from holding your partner's hand at a café to hitting the hay together toward the night's end. These gestures do not only show how you feel about your partner, but they also indicate that you are proud and appreciative of them.

## 7. Get familiar with your partner's behavior

Does your partner wish to be left alone when they are vexed? How do they react in some specific situations? These inquiries are basic, however the responses to them will enable you to comprehend the behavior of your partner — and prevent you from offending them accidentally. The way your partner views the world is not the same way you do, so the way they act in situations will most likely differ as well.

## 8. Learn when to apologize

You need to realize that being correct isn't as significant as being empathetic. Though clashes occur in a relationship, few arguments are a test that should be won. What I am trying to pass across is simple — know what is worth fighting for and when you need to accept the blame. It is better to say sorry than turn a small argument into a relationship-breaking crisis.

## Practical Lessons and Exercises

A healthy relationship makes life better.

Think, for a moment, of the stress and suffering that you experience when you live with a conflict. Thus, your life is improved when you aim for harmony in your relationship.

This exercise is a form of self-diagnosis that will help you to know more specifically what to improve to bring harmony.

I encourage you to take the exercises together with your partner by your side, and to then use the evaluation to discuss ways to improve.

Note a percentage between 0% and 100% next to each of the following aspects (0% being never or little and 100% always or a lot):

Relational dimensions of you as a couple

- Your ability to speak and participate in exchanges:

- Your ability to listen to each other:

- Your ability to be empathetic (put yourself in the other person's shoes and make an effort to understand their point of view):

- Your ability to support each other through difficulties:

- Your ability to express your gratitude, your love, etc.:

- Your ability to approach the subject of your relationship with the other in order to improve it:

Once you have established a percentage, focus on improving those with the lowest score.

Questions to identify the strengths and weaknesses of your relationship

The answers to each of these questions will help you to become aware of the positive elements of your relationship for which you can maintain gratitude as well as identify any gaps that you can work on together.

- What do you like most about your relationship?:

- What are you missing? What are you not satisfied with?:

- What is your degree of intimacy and affection as a couple?:

- Does this degree satisfy you?:

Having answered those questions, here are some more strategies to help you nurture your desire to be happy in your relationship and to make your love last. The good news is that it is possible. Of course, it involves hard work, it won't always feel like magic, but it is quite possible to develop new skills and be happy together.

## 1. Be in love with yourself

It is impossible to be happy as a couple if you're not happy with yourself first. Love is first and foremost to be offered to yourself. Fall in love with your own life.

Be happy with the person you are. Know yourself and to accept yourself as you are. Develop a beautiful intimacy with your inner world. Feel confident, strong, and proud to be who you are. It's a challenge, but it's also fundamental! Learn to savor your own presence.

The more you are rich in your own life and you are bathed in energy of benevolence towards yourself, the more your love for others will be true and profound. Thus, you can say without hesitation that the love you offer is proportional to the love you have for yourself. Without this first movement of gratitude and tenderness towards yourself, you risk looking for a partner to fill your void or the lack you see in yourself. Two whole people coming together makes for a better relationship than two people looking to fill a void.

## 2. Love is a commitment more than a feeling

Love in a healthy and sustainable relationship is more than butterflies in the belly and sparks in the eyes. Too often, we have an idyllic vision of romantic love. It is thought that love at first sight is the guarantee of a relationship that will last forever. That passion must be maintained at all costs, in total intensity, otherwise we conclude that love is no more and that the break is inevitable.

In reality, true love doesn't come from a chemical reaction in the brain or hormones gone crazy. It comes from dedicated effort to appreciate each other even when it feels like the "spark" is no longer there.

True love is able to pass from the exalted feelings in the beginning to a solid and stable companionship in daily, ordinary life. Investing in a happy and nurturing relationship requires effort, determination, and perseverance.

It is important to remember that love meets one of our basic needs: to feel safe emotionally. Thus, when love is the result of mutual commitment, it becomes very safe. This security allows you and your partner to stand together through the trials of life and know that you each have someone to lean on.

### 3. Investing in the relationship

A committed love is a love where you invest deeply in the relationship. One could compare the relationship to a plant. If we want it to be beautiful and healthy, we must take care of it (water it, put it in the light, repot it occasionally, etc.).

The same goes for relationships. You must maintain it to keep it alive and allow it to grow and evolve. Too often, couples end their relationship because they have not cared for it enough. It is not love that has failed, it is effort. This is a problem of negligence. Like the plant, an unmaintained relationship fades, withers, and eventually dies.

To succeed in your relationships, it is essential to devote time and energy into them. Too easily we take the other person for granted. We get bogged down in the routine and business of life. The schedule is so full that there is no more room to simply take time to share and be together. This inevitably creates emotional impoverishment and weakens the connection.

Here are some pointers to nourish your relationship:

- Every day, take at least 30 minutes to discuss your day and mood (In person, not through text).

- Do special activities as a couple at least once a month.

- Work on projects together.

- Take care of each other with small touches, delicacies, and surprises.

- Regularly express your gratitude, your affection, and your commitment to your loved one.

## 4. Authentic Communication

Effective communication is an essential key to the success of a fulfilling love life. The more you and your lover create an emotional climate of trust and security between yourselves, the more self-revelations will be possible. But it is, among other things, the depth of the exchanges that binds the both of you together and encourages intimacy. You can talk about the rain and good weather with your colleagues and friends, but aim for something more meaningful with your partner.

This type of sharing imbued with authenticity and depth brings the both of you closer together by allowing you to feel solidarity with each other and be connected. This deep connection is certainly one of the main goals of a married life - feeling emotionally connected to each other which you can cherish more than anything.

Some strategies that promote communication:

- Take responsibility for your life.

- Avoid at all costs accusing your partner.

- Share your emotions and clearly express your needs. Don't make the other person guess.

- Express empathy and compassion for what your partner tells you.

- Really listen to your partner -don't prepare a response, just listen to hear.

- Avoid taboo subjects. They poison the relationship.

## 5. Admire your partner

Believe in your partner's potential and support them while they work to implement their dreams. Whether it is 5 or 30 years that you walk together, the goal is the same - to be there for each other.

Maintain a positive view of who your partner is and who they are becoming. This movement of profound complicity allows couples to accompany each other in their quest for happiness and a meaningful existence.

I know the challenge is great. Too easily, you begin to see only what gets on your nerves, but try to never lose sight of the overall picture.

Love is a commitment that requires a lot of investment, maturity, and will. In marital matters, we are all far from experts.

You have to make a choice to criticize your partner very rarely and, instead, to regularly acknowledge their accomplishments. Choose to see the glass half full and not half empty, and appreciate your partner.

The "perfect" partner, like the perfect human, does not exist. The life of a couple is a perpetual dance of compromise, adjustments, and letting go.

Happiness comes from making a bouquet with the flowers that we have.

## 6. Change yourself rather than changing your partner

There is no greater or crueler mirror to show us our flaws than a relationship. While the other person may bring out the best in you, they also may inadvertently cause you to notice the worst. This goes both ways - we often don't recognize our flaws until someone else sees them. It is difficult to submit to the vulnerability that comes from being in a relationship and realizing we're not perfect.

Sometimes, we use this vulnerability in our partner and use it to try to change what we don't like rather than focusing on what we can change about ourselves. Our pride tends to ally itself with our ego to comfortably indulge in denial and blindness.

Obviously, wanting to change another person is a futile wish. You only have power over yourself. It is up to you to do the work of healing and transforming yourself. Relationships can become a wonderful opportunity to heal your own wounds, even if it's terribly scary to go where it hurts.

What if you turned your gaze to yourself rather than blame the other person? What if you recognized that you can do more good for the relationship by focusing on yourself?

## 7. Choose your arguments wisely

Let's be realistic - it's inevitable in such an intimate relationship, which affects so many spheres of life, that there will be tensions over the ways of seeing and doing things. Life with another person works to exacerbate the differences. It is utopian to aspire to harmony and perfect agreement in all areas. There will be struggles - but they're not all bad.

So, how do you argue in a healthy way?

- Remember that the other is your lover and not your enemy.

- Work as a team and not as opponents.

- Do not declare war but look for "win-win" solutions.

- Avoid sterile dynamics: "Who is wrong and who is right?"

- Defuse conflicts early before they escalate.

- Avoid words that destroy: revenge, hatred,

punishment.

- Your romantic life as lovers is a dance for two, not a boxing fight.

- See the differences as an enrichment and not as an obstacle.

- Nourish the bond of secure attachment, even at the heart of tensions

- Address conflicts calmly and gently. This greatly increases the chances of positive resolutions.

## 8. Power is worth sharing

One of the major issues in life for two comes from power. We want it. We aspire to it. We hold it. We demand to be seen, heard, recognized, and to take our place in the world - the one that belongs to us right. We fight to claim our space.

You and your partner exist in and share the same territory. This creates an inevitable power struggle if you don't view the partnership as a joint effort. This can, in some cases, be healthy and balanced, but in some couples the struggle for power becomes toxic and destructive. The supposed partners of the same team become enemies. They play against each other. The duo becomes a duel. When a couple bickers frequently about something as trivial as how to place dishes in the dishwasher, the issue is not the dishes, but the power.

The distribution of power is found in many dimensions of everyday life. The division of tasks is a very sensitive place. It is one of the first sources of conflict for couples. Moreover, several surveys show that couples who have a balanced division of labor are more likely to last in love. It is a question of justice and equity.

## 9. Love is human

Why is it so hard to love? Why so many separations? What makes cohabitation with a loved one so demanding? Multiple factors explain the high recurrence of difficulty when it comes to success in a relationship. It seems important to me to highlight one: our dilemma between our animal side and our human side.

Although we humans claim to be very advanced and superior to all other creations of the earth, we must not forget that the animal in us is never too far away. Part of our brain, the hypothalamus, which we call the reptilian brain, is programmed to ensure our survival. Survival depends on protection against dangers. In your relationship, your partner may sometimes be perceived as a danger.

Your survival mechanism calls for the protection of your territory. No doubt, we are biologically programmed to respond to our own needs and to react negatively to anything that could threaten our way of life.

Fortunately, you have also been endowed with a rational and emotional intelligence. At the heart of your humanity, your nature is fundamentally good, caring, and loving. Is it not the ultimate evolution of the human being to be loved?

You can choose which of the two sides you prioritize. Which will win? To walk towards the best of yourself requires a great opening of awareness and presence to your inner issues. To truly love, you must first undertake the great job of healing your own love wounds and defensive scars. This process of transformation makes it possible to acquire a greater maturity, both emotionally and psychologically. This maturity is certainly an essential ingredient for a healthy and sustainable married life. Choose the human side, and choose to put love first.

## 10. Avoid the worst things you could do

It seems to me essential to conclude with the things to avoid at all costs in a relationship.

Do not criticize, accuse, or humiliate your partner when you're fighting. This only adds fuel to the fire and acts as a declaration of war. In this game, there are only losers. There is a way to manage tensions without destroying yourself and falling prey to your lowest instincts.

Watch out for excessively violent words. They leave marks that often cannot be gotten rid of. It takes a few seconds to utter them, but months, if not years, to heal their wounds.

It is not profitable to escape tensions by silence or choosing to sulk. These withdrawal attitudes only exacerbate the situation. They damage rather than improve the connection. The classic scenario in unhealthy relationship dynamics often resembles the following: The woman expresses her discontent, and the man stops listening and withdraws into his cave.

The more the man withdraws, the more frustration accumulate. The more the woman manifests her distress, the more the man becomes isolated, and so on, progressing until it blows up. This all too common pattern leads to a debilitating toxic spiral. The communication no longer exists. The couple is transformed into two solitudes that suffer. When this cycle is chronic, it can mark the beginning of the end.

We are fundamentally beings of relationships and love. We are made to love and to be loved. The life of a couple is certainly a privileged place to experience a secure and nourishing intimacy. Research has proven that couples are happier and enjoy better physical and psychological health. It is worthwhile to believe in it and invest in a healthy relationship!

# Chapter 7: Cultivating New and Healthy Relationships

Love has its own pitfalls. What at the beginning usually looks like a life on a cuddly cloud can quickly change into conflict and struggle. Love is not just the feeling of having butterflies in your stomach. Maintaining true love is hard work, but in the end it is well paid for with happiness and satisfaction. The following tips can help you to have a relationship that elegantly bypasses the typical points of friction. Read how to recognize and nurture real love.

Being in love changes people in their attitude and behavior. It's intoxicating, exciting, and scary all at the same time. Love is not the feeling of lust and delusion. Love is something more in every sense of feeling.

## Allow vulnerability

One of the first signs of being in love is when you

become suddenly very vulnerable. This vulnerability is present in your feelings, longings, and fear. When you begin to fall in love, your heart will open to your partner. You begin to entrust your heart to your partner and show yourself to them, as you do only with very close people.

You may be worried about being vulnerable, especially if you've had bad experiences in previous relationships. When you are open and vulnerable, those issues that were otherwise suppressed by you can come into your consciousness in new relationships. Therein lies the fear that is often justified - but don't allow it to scare you away. New relationships are just that - new. Judging them based on past experience isn't fair to you or them.

True beauty comes from within

Another sure sign of falling in love is the ability to see the inner beauty of a person. At the beginning of a romantic relationship, much attention is paid to the exterior.

Over time, as the feelings of love blossom, you will see the true personality of your counterpart - their true inner beauty. At this thought, the saying "love makes you blind" is confirmed.

## The family

If you are in a relationship with someone who one day asks you if they can meet your family, you can be sure that the person is falling in love with you or even deeply in love with you. The family is very important, and getting to know the family of your partner makes the seriousness of the relationship clear. If you have been introduced to both the family and the circle of friends, you can be sure that the feelings of your partner are genuine.

## Selflessness

The last and clearest sign of falling in love is pure selflessness. This happens when you or your partner put the needs of both of you in the foreground and subordinate your own needs.

You do everything in your power to be sure that the other person is happy. It gives your partner the feeling of being cared for, which in turn makes you happy because you have seen and fulfilled the needs of your lover.

A one-sided relationship does not help you. Even if you feel that you cannot live without your partner and love them beyond measure, if the both of you aren't on the same page, the relationship will go nowhere. Here are some ways to cultivate meaningful and healthy relationships in the early stages:

## 1. Be clear about what you need

On your first date, before your entrées have even touched the table, the both of you should examine what you truly want for from a relationship. Be clear about what you are looking for. This way, you will both be on the same page from the get go. The idea of this can be alarming, but in any case learn to expect the unexpected. They just might disclose similar wishes.

## 2. Talk about your dreams and wants

Would you like to build a small home and live off the grid? Take a year off to travel the far reaches of the planet? Write a book? Share these dreams with a potential partner. Discover whether your objectives compliment another person's and if you have overlapping interests. It's far more fun to find out about someone when discussing dreams rather than general hobbies.

## 3. Have wide open communication

If something is troubling you, do not hold it inside because of a paranoid fear of what may occur if you bring it up. Address the issues and have quiet, caring discussions to see the two points of view. It's such a much needed refresher to know you both want to cooperate to discuss anything before something turns into a major issue. It's not about being right or wrong — it's about the two individuals working together.

163

## 4. Accept each aspect of yourself

If you don't accept yourself for who you are, why should someone else? There may be aspects of yourself that you don't like or would change if you could, but they aren't important. The sooner you can look at yourself and be happy with everything you see, the better of you'll be in life and in love.

## 5. Manage stress together

Stress will never leave — it's the means with which we handle it that matters. When your partner is disturbed or stressed, be there for them to vent to. Don't attempt to fix it all; rather, allow them to work through the problem as they wish to. All they need is to know that you're there.

## 6. Offer thanks regularly

Having a mutual appreciation for each other is massively beneficial. It's also important to give thanks for other aspects of your life. Grateful people are happy people, and a couple that is grateful for each other is better able to build a healthy relationship.

## 7. Talk about the big things

Talk about everything, from moving in together to building a home, from children to funds and family travels. Don't wait until these events are here - get a head start and begin discussing your expectations early. Many couples dread this sort of talk for fear that their partner will not agree with them. But the sooner you uncover differences, the sooner you can begin working to come to a compromise.

## 8. Have dinner together

People bond over shared food, so make the most of it! Put on some romantic music, dress nicely, and connect. The meal almost doesn't matter as much as the full, undivided attention of the both of you.

## 9. Be available

When you need your partner, do you want them to be available, or will you be able to deal with them prioritizing something else over you? If you wish to be put first, start by putting them first. Be ready to come to their aid if they need you. You don't have to drop everything on a whim, but ensure you know what you're going to do if they ever let you know that they're going through a crisis and could use your support. Your actions in their time of need set the tone for the future.

## 10. Work toward being a better partner

If you're like most people, there are things you wish to change about yourself. Some of these desired changes can positively affect your relationship. By striving to be the best person you can be for the one you love, you're also becoming better for yourself.

You don't need to settle. You can develop your relationship and make it something that persistently improves your life. A happy relationship resembles everything you adore; you should be focused on learning, developing, and continually hoping to improve.

Always remember that it's okay to argue. Numerous investigations demonstrate that couples who disagree have more beneficial connections. For a long time I considered arguments to be a disappointment, yet in all actuality they are important aspects of a solid relationship. To argue with consideration for each other means that you're invested.

A solid relationship is two people cooperating to build a life together. A solid relationship is somewhat similar to a trinity, two people make something more profound and superior to themselves, yet they are still themselves. For a relationship to develop, you should likewise develop as an individual and not lose yourself.

## Enjoy being in love

Are you newly in love? Then you are probably feeling great right now! I have a few good tips for you to help you get the most out of your love and keep it strong for a long time.

First, take enough space and time to enjoy your love. This means you may have less time for your existing circle of friends. Your friends will certainly understand this and be happy with you, as long as it does not become a long term trend. Your friends are important, too.

Do things you've wanted to do for a long time. Through shared experiences, you and your partner grow together all the more. The base of a relationship is largely made up of shared experiences.

Go out together:

- to the theater

- to a concert

- to the cinema

- to the opera

Also get to know your partner's friends, and ensure your partner is introduced to your friends. Acceptance in the mutual circle of friends also says a lot about how you as a couple harmonize together.

Visit friends or invite them over, and ensure they don't feel like you or your partner are cutting them out.

Additionally, talks should not be neglected despite the romance. Celebrate your shared romance, because it gives strength for less good times and creates a great common ground. Conversations are just as important as experiences, though. Share your feelings with your partner and give them the opportunity to get to know you as well.

## Tips for a long and happy relationship

The following tips will help keep your relationship healthy for a long time.

### Avoid nagging

Any kind of criticism of your partner's idiosyncrasies either leads to quarrels or makes you feel annoyed. Psychologists are of the opinion that criticizing your partner in many cases is a projection of your own shortcomings.

Rather than frustrating your partner with complaints, you might think about what makes you uncomfortable about their traits, and work on reframing your viewpoint.

### *Understand that your partner is their own personality*

You must accept the fact that your partner is an individual with a unique personality. Nevertheless, we subconsciously and sometimes consciously treat our partner as if they are an extension of ourselves. Accept that your partner is a being with a character of their own with appropriate feelings and perceptions, opinions, and experiences.

### *Accept your partner's mistakes*

To err is human. Your partner is not an angel, so they are bound to make mistakes. When that happens, learn to forgive and do not capitalize on the mistakes of your partner.

Above all, there are lots of things we cannot change about our partner, so rather than grumbling or nagging, why not learn to live with them? Small mistakes are not a matter of life and death. If you find it difficult to cope with your partner's idiosyncrasies, call their attention to it, and explain yourself in a polite manner. Don't blame or accuse, simply discuss.

### Do not tolerate destructive behavior

Learn to tolerate your partner as long as their behavior is not destructive or life threatening. If you discover that your spouse or partner is very aggressive, don't paint over the situation and learn to "cope." Your safety is important. If you ever feel threatened, don't stick around to try to keep the peace. Get out.

### Take emotional time out

Our skin needs sunlight for the production of vitamin D. However, prolonged and frequent sunbathing can cause life-threatening skin cancer.

So the right dosage is important. This applies to relationships, as well.

Of course, we need each other to fill our lives with happiness. But, we also need emotional time-outs in which one does not think of the other person or is involved in the planning of joint activities.

Meet alone with friends or join a club alone to develop yourself as a person. If both partners experience something different from each other, there is also something to talk about at the dinner table.

### Do not tie conditions to gifts

A gift is a gift. And a favor is a favor. In a marriage or intimate relationship, you should never attach any condition to a gift or favor. If you want to do something good for your partner, then go ahead without any ulterior motive.

Do not make a game like "I'll give you a massage if you give me one." The same applies to the prices of gifts. Just because you have given your partner a computer, that does not mean they have to express their affection with something equally expensive.

Accept favors and gifts for what they are: gestures and symbols of love. Incidentally, this also applies to compliments.

We often tend not to take the compliments and praise from our partners seriously. But just because your partner loves you, that do not make their opinion worthless. If your partner tells you that you're pretty, then accept the compliment and do not disappoint them by dismissing it with an "Oh, that's just what you say."

### Be honest

Honesty is the best policy. Not only is this concept over two centuries old, but it exactly hits the point where relationships can fail.

Half-truths and lies cannot be kept secret for long if you aim to live a peacefully together with your partner. Also, do not hide any material facts that could have a direct impact on the growing relationship. For example, if you have children from a previous relationship, that's something that will have to come out eventually.

### Be faithful and sincere

Unless you have made other arrangements, share a duvet exclusively with your romantic partner and no one else. To be deceived and cheated on by a close person is one of the cruelest experiences that can happen to anyone.

If you really love your partner, you will spare them that experience. Ultimately, faithfulness builds such deep trust that you can't replace or fix it once broken.

### Address problems

No partnership is in complete harmony. You are two different personalities with thoughts and feelings. A relationship, no matter how much love and dedication you feel for each other, is always the result of many compromises.

Instead of holding long-standing resentments, you should discuss issues openly with your partner and work together to find a solution without immediately interpreting them as signs of a nonfunctional relationship. Precisely because you are able to talk about difficult points, you have a strong partnership.

Bear in mind that nobody can read your mind. A certain amount of empathy is to be expected, but over relying on it can lead to misunderstandings.

Therefore, face critical matters head on rather than waiting for the other to address the problem. Couples therapists unanimously agree that communication is the key to a long, healthy, and fulfilling relationship.

### Appreciate what you see in your partner

The first infatuation does not disappear forever. Most of the time it gives way only to another feeling, that of deep attachment and love.

You have found that you can rely on your partner. That they think of you, and in so many ways suit you perfectly. That you as a couple harmonize and like to be with one another.

These are all the things you have always dreamed of. Now that they have become reality, are you taking the time to appreciate them fully?

Consider your partner once from these points of view, and you will see how happy you are to have them. Show your partner some of that happiness and gratitude. Talk to them about your feelings, and you will see the old familiar infatuation soon building again.

### Romantic excursions

Enjoy your closeness, and take out time for romantic excursions from everyday life. Take a nice walk in the fall, or have a special dinner together in the evening. Everyday life can dull us to the magic that is being with another person. Get away from the routine to rediscover your partner.

For a relationship to work, you have to do a lot for it.

## Why love turns to work

True love. That's what we long for until we actually

find them. This special person who understands us without words and knows us better than anyone else, a person who accepts us, flaws and all, such a person shows genuine love. What sounds like an unachievable reverie can actually come true.

### After Cloud 9 comes the harsh reality

We all experience similar feelings from a new love in the first few weeks and months of dating. It feels like true love has been found - the great love that makes life worth living.

But then, many of them land on the ground of reality rather roughly when the first difficulties arise in the romantic relationship. True love does not survive by itself, but involves real work.

### When the effect of "drug love" subsides

Love involves, more than anything else, chemical reactions. These chemicals can make us rather irrational in the beginning when we're discovering more about someone else and falling deeper in love.

Unfortunately, the drug called love loses its chemical action after some time. Our body is designed to get used to stimuli. And so our brain gets used to the high-making messengers, which slowly but surely lose their effect and the rosy glasses gradually turn clear again.

### Fall in love again and again

Incidentally, it is by no means the case that the said messengers are only distributed at the beginning of a romance. Certain shared experiences, such as the birth of a child or a romantic vacation, can also trigger the payout.

Just because the tingling sensation has disappeared, that does not mean that you no longer feel love for your partner. Just use ingenuity to make yourself fall in love with your better half over and over again.

There are some behaviors that get in the way of "falling in love again," however.

# Errors in love affairs

During periods of turmoil, people in relationships sometimes have irrational thoughts or ideas that don't help the relationship, their partner, or themselves. Some of these notions include:

### You absolutely need a partner to be happy

There are singles who are desperately looking for a partner because they think - or, as in most cases, have heard - that it is essential to have someone by their side to be happy. If you do not have that, life is much less fun and you feel alone and somehow worthless.

Of course, such a statement is not universal, if only for the reason that every person is different and thus their version of "happiness" will be different. However, the fact is that you can feel good even without a permanent partner - and whoever radiates this outwardly will immediately be more attractive to a potential new love.

### A child can save a relationship

It is not a good idea to think that a child will improve your relationship. Children are wonderful, but they put a relationship under new challenges and stress.

If a relationship is already fraught with conflict, then you should think very carefully about the desire to have a baby, or wait a little longer so that you have fewer conflicts with your partner. Children are only enriching when their parents are aware that they will have less time for each other, themselves, and more financial responsibility.

### Dependencies do not make you happy

Do not commit the mistake and put all positive experiences and feelings into the relationship with your partner. Keep in mind at the beginning of the relationship as well as further in that it is you who has to make yourself happy. Do not give the responsibility to your partner and do not make yourself dependent on them to be happy.

Preserve the ability to be responsible for yourself and your happiness. In this way, your relationship will grow easier and be more stable, and you both will be happier knowing one isn't relying on the other.

### Relationship and sex don't necessarily belong together

The importance of having sex in a partnership varies from person to person. There are couples who live their sex life very passionately and often, while others are rarely intimate, but still romantic.

It is important that both sides are happy with the level of intimacy and that you acknowledge the needs of each other. If you have problems in this regard, you should not shy away from an open conversation. Just remember that if you're both happy with the way things are, but the influences of the media and society tell you it should be different, listen to your heart. Only the two of you know what's right for your relationship.

## Talking to a New Partner about Your Anxiety

Anxiety is a medical condition, and as such you shouldn't be ashamed of it. While you don't have to tell anyone about your anxiety if you don't want to, knowing the ways it can affect you will help your partner learn how to help you. If you ever are in a situation that makes you uncomfortable and you haven't talked to your partner about it before, it becomes that much more difficult to manage the situation. If you've decided it will be beneficial to discuss your anxiety with a new partner, here are some tips:

### Start by Explaining What Anxiety Means to You

Anxiety doesn't look the same for every sufferer. While your partner may know what anxiety is, they will not know what it's like in your specific situation. You may be fine with crowds, but intimate gatherings make you uncomfortable. Or, you may only be able to go to certain restaurants that are familiar to you. However anxiety manifests itself in your life, tell your

182

partner. The more they know, the more they can help you.

### *Go Over Your Symptoms*

Your partner might not be able to recognize an anxiety attack when it happens. Let them know what happens when your anxiety is triggered. Do you become short of breath, begin to pass out, or become irritable? Whatever happens to you, let them know, no matter how embarrassing. If you need help in a specific situation and they are the only one there with you who knows about your anxiety, you want to ensure they can recognize the signs that you are about to have an attack.

### *Tell Them about Your Triggers*

Give them a full list, even if it's long. There are things they will be able to avoid, and situations they will be able to steer you away from. Bring them into your world and let them see life from your perspective by letting them know what seemingly innocent aspects of the world make your heart pound and your palms sweat. Believe it or not, this can help the two of you grow closer.

### Let Them Know How They Can Help

Rest assured, they will want to help you. At least, they will if they're a keeper. After showing them what anxiety looks like in your life, give them the tools to help you if need be. Tell them what calms you down, what steps need to be taken in a given situation to prevent an attack, and how they can support you as you work to control your anxiety.

# Chapter 8: You Deserve a Wholesome Relationship

You deserve somebody who will love you unconditionally. Somebody who won't renege on their promise to remain with you when you are down with depression or anxiety, someone who won't run away when things get difficult, and somebody who won't abandon you when you need them the most.

Hold out for somebody who takes delight in treating you right. Somebody who can really meet your standards. Somebody who can offer you the respect you deserve and also offer you complete honesty.

Someone that deserves your time is a person who won't just say that they have strong feelings for you - they take steps to prove those words. Somebody who can put in effort to arrange dates and share secrets and sometimes be romantic, somebody who will do whatever it takes to keep your relationship strong.

A person who is worth dating is somebody who can cause you to feel loved every moment, not someone who causes you to wonder whether or not their feelings have ceased. Natural anxiety is one thing - anxiety caused by an absent partner is another.

Be with someone who provides out their loving attention freely without your having to ask for it. Be with someone who isn't afraid to inform the planet how lucky they feel to have you or how precious you are.

A person who loves you despite (or maybe because of) all your flaws is not someone that you should let go. Somebody who accepts that you simply are the sort of person who overthinks and overreacts and does what they can to calm your fears is worth keeping around.

You should hesitate to invest your care and affection in someone who holds back their love. Instead, find somebody who grabs your hand and kisses you in public, no matter who is watching, treats you tenderly, and says I love you each and every time they feel the urge.

You deserve unlimited love from someone who is happy to be by your side for the rest of your lives.

Of course, never neglect the love you receive from your friends and relations. You should surround yourself with those that bring out the best in you, not those that tear you down, magnify your flaws, or make you feel like you are not progressing.

Most of all, you have to love yourself. You might have anxiety, worry often, and overthink most situations - but that's no reason to dislike who you are. Quit criticizing yourself in ways you'd never dream of criticizing anyone else. Stop thinking there's one thing horrifically wrong with you, and that if you change that thing life will be better. Don't be any less than who you are - you. You deserve happiness and a wholesome relationship, but you have to fall in love with yourself first.

In spite of what you have been through or believed, you deserve love, affection, and a fulfilling relationship.

## What makes a healthy relationship?

But what's a healthy relationship? There are so many qualities and factors behind the emotions and actions that structure healthy relationships. However, all extraordinary romances share one thing: they're the results of commitment to the continued mastery of relationship skills.

Daily applications of those skills is important. Developing the habits and patterns to make and maintain a rare relationship needs acute self-awareness and application and repetition of excellent behavior and communication. Once these habits are established between you and your partner, the fulfilling, healthy relationship you deserve can follow and endure.

What will a healthy relationship look like? It's two individuals creating one unique and loving life together. The more effort you both put into this, the more fulfilling the link becomes. What are your partner's core desires? Comfort? Security? Significance? How can these needs best be met?

Practice the foundational ability to understand, and use that understanding to create a powerful partnership.

### *Develop the link you desire*

As you think about what makes a healthy relationship, bear in mind that understanding your partner's desires involves communicating effectively with them. You don't have to be a mind reader in a relationship. Take to heart what has been discussed in this book and learn to talk with them about their needs and wants. Remember, listening is not about you – it's about what you'll be able to do for the person you love.

Once you recognize the desires of both you and your partner, you'll be able to actively work to ensure positive expectations are met. What are you doing for the love of your life? Something, right? Meeting your significant other's core desires can take you to profound levels of happiness, love, passion, and trust.

What if the road ahead is hard and packed with challenges? Issues, obstacles and problems present opportunities to grow closer. You've heard of the phrase, "They got too comfortable," haven't you? If you're just comfortable in your relationship, you almost certainly aren't growing or changing. Lack of growth is referred to as stagnation, which might cause deterioration when it involves a relationship. Growth ensures relationships continue to evolve with the people in them.

None of this implies that you have to point out the flaws in each other in order to grow and change. On the contrary, appreciating your partner the way they are is what makes a relationship strong. Those flaws are a part of the person you love - they could even be part of the reason you fell in love with them in the first place. Appreciate them completely, flaws and all. After all, don't you hope they'll do the same for you?

### *Trust yourself - and your partner*

Trust is the foundation of all productive and healthy relationships. From trust springs respect, and each measure is necessary for sharing, interaction, and growth. And it's throughout times of stress and uncertainty, when your mutual commitment will be subject to doubt, that you discover how much you trust each other. Will your partner trust you to be there for them, even once you're stressed or uncertain? Will your partner trust you to be honest and clear with them, even if what you have to say may hurt? Do they trust that you can meet their needs?

Once you are able to cultivate a healthy relationship, here are 10 wonderful benefits you will receive:

## Support

Have you ever wanted to start a business? How about write a book, or travel the world? Maybe you just want to start a family and do everything you can to raise loving children. In a healthy relationship, you can dive into any one of your goals or dreams and feel secure knowing that you have unwavering support in the form of your partner. Nothing chases away anxiety like a supportive partner!

## Inspiration

Chances are, you're a pretty amazing person. Being an amazing person, you will naturally attract someone who is also fantastic. You know what's great about being the kind of people you both are? You're bound to inspire one another! While you will both be supportive of one another, as stated above, some of your more ambitious activities just might inspire the same kind of ambition in your partner and vice versa. You will be able to reach new heights thanks to the loving support and inspirational guidance provided by a special partner.

## Better Health

Studies show that healthy relationships offer a multitude of health benefits, from lowering blood pressure to strengthening the immune system.

Sounds like a good deal, doesn't it? Perhaps the new saying will go something like "A kiss from you true love a day keeps the doctor away!"

## Encouragement

Along with the emotional support your partner offers you, they will also encourage you in your endeavors. They will be overjoyed to see you succeed and thus will do all they can to ensure you do. We all need encouragement every now and again, even when we're big strong adults who can take care of ourselves. Everyone wants to hear someone else say that they can succeed. A partner is your personal cheerleader, and you are theirs. Encourage each other to be all you can both be.

## Longer Life

While health benefits are great on their own, the greatest aspect of a loving relationship is the likelihood that you will live longer. Studies have revealed that healthy partnerships slow down aging and reduce the chances of couples developing age-related diseases, leading to an increased life expectancy. Better find someone you can spend the next 50+ years with.

## Affection

Humans crave affection. Even babies know the power of a mother's touch. Having a partner means having a constant source of affection. When you're sad, happy, angry, or just in need of a hand to hold, you know where to turn. Knowing that the other person will be there to provide the affection you crave is powerful.

## Sense of Purpose

You don't need someone else to give your life meaning, but having someone around who provides support and encouragement makes it a lot easier to face life with a sense of vigor. Pursuing your goals and searching for your life's meaning become more important when you share your life with someone, because in order for the relationship to be at its best, both of you need to be at your best.

## Friendship

It's so important that your partner or spouse also be your friend. Love, intimacy, and passion will only last so long. At the end of the day, it might be more important to like the person you're with than love them. Having a deep and caring friendship first and foremost will help you build a stronger foundation for the romantic relationship, which can suffer from hardships and difficulties that won't affect the friendship that lies underneath.

## Less Stress

This might not always be true - after all, even healthy relationships have their conflicts. But on the whole, loving relationships lead to less stress. This may be due to several reasons, from the sharing of responsibilities and finances to the calming effects of intimacy. Whatever the reason, sharing your life with someone will not bring on more drama, as some may believe. When you prioritize each other and work to build a lasting relationship, stress melts away.

## Love

It's obvious, but must be stated regardless. What we are after when we begin a relationship is love. It might seem like a simple thing to find, but the pages of history and novels teach us that it is anything but. When you cultivate a meaningful friendship and subsequently a healthy relationship, you are rewarded with the most wonderful gift on Earth - the love of another human being.

# Conclusion

Love is enjoyable when you let go of the anxiety that comes between you and your partner. When you give anxiety a chance to run free in your love life, it may be difficult to know when and how to react to some sensitive situations. This may lead you to feel indifferent or unconcerned to some vital relationship issues, or put on a show of being uninvolved and forceful when speaking with your partner. While it's certainly not your fault, it's beneficial to understand how anxiety may be affecting the manner in which you see things.

When it feels like anxiety is genuinely keeping you down, you will need to overcome it both for your well-being and for the health of your relationship. By reading this book and putting all the tips and techniques into action, you will be able to overcome every anxiety and insecurity in your relationship. The strategies in this book aim to help you learn positive adapting attitudes to managing your anxiety in the right manner, and that can mean having a more advantageous relationship by maintaining a strategic distance from certain anxiety related errors.

Anxiety is love's most noteworthy executioner. It makes others feel as if you are suffocating them. It's not easy to overcome this, but it's possible.

Anxiety makes it hard to realize what's important and what's not. It can blow things out of proportion, distract us, and cripple us. But it doesn't have to control us.

You deserve to be in a happy, loving relationship that isn't marred by anxiety's vicious grip. All it takes is conscious effort and a new perspective to realize that anxiety's weakness is a loving connection. By strengthening your relationship, you weaken anxiety's grasp. What's a better example of a win-win than that?

# References

Baglan. A.(n.d)..15 Conscious choices to cultivate the relationship you want from day one. Retrieved from https://www.google.com/amp/s/amp.mindbodygreen.com/articles/15-conscious-choices-to-cultivate-the-relationship-you-want-from-day-one--22429

Clark. A.(2019, January 4).When a relationship causes anxiety. Retrieved from https://aliciaclarkpsyd.com/when-a-relationship-causes-anxiety/

Janice. M (2017, Dec. 6) Retrieved from https://www.google.com/amp/s/m.huffpost.com/us/entry/9220678/amp

Matty.M. (2017, July 1) How to Resolve Conflict in a Relationship Retrieved from https://pairedlife.com/problems/How-to-Resolve-Conflicts-in-Relationships

Selma (2017, Dec. 9) 11 things you deserve from a

relationship. Retrieved from
https://thinkaloud.net/2017/12/09/11-things-you-deserve-from-a-relationship/

Smith. K.(n.d) Anxiety Romantic Relationship.
Retrieved from https://www.psycom.net/anxiety-romantic-relationships/

CPSIA information can be obtained
at www.ICGtesting.com
Printed in the USA
BVHW061724220321
603180BV00002B/185